Eyes Open 3

STUDENT'S BOOK

Ben Goldstein & **Ceri Jones**
with **Vicki Anderson** & **Eoin Higgins**

CAMBRIDGE
UNIVERSITY PRESS

DISCOVERY
EDUCATION

Starter Unit

Meeting people

1 🔊 **1.01** Complete the conversation with the words in the box. Then listen, check and repeat.

> See   I'm   This   Goodbye   ~~My~~
> your   is   Pleased   Her   from

Kieran:	Hello. ¹ _My_ name's Kieran. What's ² …. name?
Fay:	Hi, Kieran. I'm Fay. ³ …. is my friend. ⁴ …. name's Gulay.
Gulay:	⁵ …. to meet you Kieran!
Kieran:	Where are you ⁶ …., Gulay?
Gulay:	⁷ …. from Istanbul in Turkey.
Fay:	Gulay ⁸ …. staying at our house.
Kieran:	Well, I have to go. ⁹ …. you later!
Fay:	¹⁰ …. Kieran!

Routines

2 Match the daily routines with the pictures.

> have lunch   ~~wake up~~   get up   have dinner
> have breakfast   go to bed   have a shower
> do homework   go to school

a   _wake up_

3 Work with a partner. Use the activities in Exercise 2 to describe a typical day in your life.

I wake up at 7.30 am and I get up quickly. Then I have a shower and have breakfast at 8 am.

Free-time activities

4 Complete the free-time activities with _do_, _go_, _play_, _read_, _sing_ or _watch_.

1   _go_ cycling
2   … judo
3   … football
4   … a book
5   … swimming
6   … exercise
7   … the guitar
8   … a song
9   … basketball
10   … a film

5 Ask and answer questions about the activities in Exercise 5 with your partner.

A: _Do you go cycling at weekends?_
B: _No, I haven't got a bicycle!_

Wh- questions

6 Match the questions and the answers.

1   Where do you live?
2   How old is this car?
3   How are you today?
4   Whose birthday is it tomorrow?
5   When did you go to London?
6   What are you doing?

a   I'm fine, thanks. And you?
b   I'm waiting for the bus.
c   It's three years old.
d   We went last summer.
e   It's Cristina's. She's 14.
f   In Paris.

7 Write the words in order to make questions.

1   study / you / Where / do ?
2   old / you / are / How ?
3   like / do / TV programmes / What / watching / you ?
4   on holiday / you / Where / next summer / go / will ?
5   teacher / last year / Who / English / your / was ?
6   get / this morning / How / you / to school / did ?

8 Ask and answer the questions in Exercise 7 with your partner.

Adjectives

1 Choose the correct words to complete the sentences.

1 My brother is so (annoying)/ friendly / weird – he is always borrowing my things.

2 Frank plays the guitar – he's really **excited / interested / surprised** in music.

3 My favourite comedian is Will Ferrell – he is so **funny / moody / unfriendly**!

4 I get really **embarrassed / interested / bored** when the news comes on – I change the channel.

5 I think Sam is a bit **tired / angry / upset** after the long journey so he's not coming out tonight.

6 I find films with clowns really **cheerful / scary / impatient**. I have nightmares after watching them.

2 Work with a partner. Use the adjectives in Exercise 1 to describe the following people.

1 a friend

2 a relative (brother, sister, uncle, aunt, etc.)

3 a teacher at school

4 a famous person

My friend Gill is really impatient; she hates waiting for the bus! She's really interested in cooking.

Comparative and superlative adjectives

3 🔊 1.02 Complete the conversations about TV programmes with the comparative or superlative adjectives. Then listen and check.

1 A: I think documentaries are .... (interesting) the news.

B: Really? I don't like documentaries or the news. Cartoons are the .... (good) thing on TV, in my opinion!

2 A: I think the .... (boring) programmes on TV are chat shows – I hate them!

B: Yes, I know what you mean. But I think reality shows are the .... (bad)!

3 A: I love watching romantic films! It's much .... (relaxing) watching action films!

B: Oh no, I love action films. They are .... (exciting) romantic films and they have the .... (good) special effects!

4 Work with a partner. Use comparatives and superlatives to compare TV shows you know.

Adverbs

5 Choose the correct words to complete the sentences.

1 Tina and I spoke **quiet /**(quietly)because Niall was studying.

2 We were all **happy / happily** to see Vicky again.

3 I'm sorry. I draw very **bad / badly**. What do you think?

4 We ran **quick / quickly** but the bus left without us.

5 Everyone thought it was an **easy / easily** exam.

6 Ian speaks French very **good / well**. He lived there for a year.

7 Drive **slow / slowly** Granny. I think Susan's house is near here.

8 Be **careful / carefully** – they bite!

6 Match four of the sentences in Exercise 5 to the pictures below.

Comparative and superlative adverbs

1 David is writing about his classmates. Complete the text with the comparative and superlative adverbs of the adjectives in brackets.

So these are my classmates – we're all really different. Alice is the best in the class. She works [1] _more quickly_ (quick) than anyone else in the class. Ryan is good at Maths so he does his Maths homework [2] .... (easy). Christine does her homework [3] .... (careful) than anyone else but it takes her hours so she definitely does things [4] .... (slow). I sit beside Paola. I can draw [5] .... (good) than she can but she's really nice and she sits [6] .... (quiet) than I do.

Past simple

2 Complete the table with the past simple form of the verbs in the box.

~~watch~~ ~~leave~~ help dance get go be wash
come walk stop take eat work have see

Regular	Irregular
watched	left

3 Complete the sentences with the past simple form of the regular verbs in Exercise 2.

1 It was a lovely day so we ..._walked_.. around the park.
2 My mum .... in a cinema when she was young.
3 Tell me about the film. I .... (not) it last night because I went to bed early.
4 .... you .... Carl with his homework?
5 It was a great party and the music was amazing. We .... for hours.
6 Sorry we're late. We .... at a shop to buy some ice cream.
7 I .... my dad's car two hours ago and now it's raining!

4 Complete the news story with the past simple form of the irregular verbs in Exercise 2. Use one verb twice.

Last weekend, my family and I [1] _went_ to the mountains. It [2] .... great. We [3] .... a really good time. We [4] .... early in the morning. My cousin Gina [5] .... with us. We [6] .... some food – sandwiches and drinks – and we [7] .... under the trees in the forest. We [8] .... some beautiful birds. When we [9] .... home we [10] .... very tired but happy.

5 Write three true past simple sentences about you, your friends or your family with the verbs and the time expressions.

eat	ago
see	last week
watch	yesterday
be	last weekend
walk	last month
had	last Friday
come	yesterday morning
wash	last year
dance	

My friend Anne ate pizza last Friday.

Speaking Explaining a problem

Real talk: Do you often lose things?

1 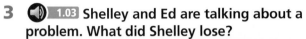 Watch the teenagers in the video. How many teens lost something once?

2 💬 Do *you* often lose things?

3 🔊 **1.03** Shelley and Ed are talking about a problem. What did Shelley lose?

4 Complete the conversation with the useful language.

Useful language

I don't know what to do.
What's the matter?
I'm not sure.
OK, don't panic!
Oh no!
For one thing (no one rang me).
Let me think …
I hope so!

Ed:	Hi, Shelley! What's the ¹ *matter* ?
Shelley:	I can't find **my school bag**! It's got **all my books** in!
Ed:	Oh ² .... ! Where did you go **after school**?
Shelley:	Umm, let me ³ .... . I went to **watch a basketball match**. After that, I **went to buy a drink**, and then we **went to the park**.
Ed:	Did you leave it **in the park**?
Shelley:	I'm ⁴ .... . I was **on my way home** when I realised I didn't have it. I went back **to the park** but I couldn't find it! I don't ⁵ .... to do!
Ed:	OK, don't ⁶ .... . Perhaps **a friend** saw it and took it **home**.
Shelley:	No, I don't think so. For one ⁷ .... , no one rang me.
Ed:	Well, maybe you left it **in the shop**. Let's go and ask if it's there.
Shelley:	OK – I ⁸ .... !

5 🔊 **1.03** Listen again and check your answers.

6 💬 Work with a partner. Practise the conversation in Exercise 4.

7 💬 Change the words in bold in the dialogue. Use the ideas below. Take turns to talk to a friend and explain what the problem is. Use the situations below or your own ideas.

Problem 1

You are at school. Your mobile isn't in your bag. It's new and was quite expensive. It has all your numbers in it and hundreds of songs. You had it this morning at home.

Problem 2

You are at a friend's house. You can't find your memory stick. It has all the work you did for a group presentation. You need it tomorrow. You had it earlier today at school.

1 Extreme living

Discovery
EDUCATION

In this unit ...

The long winter **p11**

People of the mangrove jungle **p14**

Giving your opinion **p16**

CLIL Hot topics **p115**

Vocabulary
- Extreme weather
- Words from the text
- Survival essentials
- Prepositional phrases

Language focus
- Present simple and present continuous
- Past simple and past continuous

Unit aims
I can ...
- understand a blog about extreme weather.
- describe where I live and past activities.
- understand a conversation about a news story.
- understand an article about a remote island.
- give my opinion, agree and disagree politely.
- write an email to a penfriend.

BE CURIOUS

What can you see in the photo?
Start thinking
- What do you think the man is doing?
- What is it like to live in a country with very cold weather?
- How do you think people keep warm in cold countries?

Vocabulary Extreme weather

1 🔊 **1.04** **Match the words and phrases in the box with the pictures (a–h). Then listen, check and repeat.**

> hail   boiling   freezing   heavy rain   heatwave
> thunder and lightning   snowstorm   high winds

a   *boiling*

2 **What months of the year do you think about with the weather words in Exercise 3?**

In July, it is usually boiling but in October we have heavy rain.

3 🔊 **1.05** **Listen to the radio show. Write the weather words from Exercise 3.**

1 Victor (Argentina)   *heatwave, boiling*
2 Hannah (England)
3 Oksana (Russia)
4 Silke (Germany)

➔ Say it right! • page 96

Your turn

4 **Make notes about extreme weather conditions in your country.**

5 **Work with a partner. What does he/she do in extreme weather? Then report your partner's answers to the class.**

A: What do you do when it's freezing?
B: I wear a lot of clothes and a scarf, hat and gloves.

➔ Vocabulary Bank • page 107

Reading A blog

1 **Work with a partner. Look at the photos and answer the questions.**

1 Where is Yakutsk, do you think?
2 What is special about it?

2 🔊 **1.09** **Meg is a British student at the University of Yakutsk in Siberia, Russia. Read her blog. Do you think she prefers summer or winter there?**

3 **Read Meg's blog again. Answer the questions.**

1 What is Meg doing now? *Meg is sitting indoors and writing her blog.*
2 What is the average daytime temperature in Yakutsk in winter?
3 What effect does the extreme cold have on people's bodies?
4 Why is she learning how to play kyyly?
5 How many hours of sunlight do they get in Yakutsk in summer?
6 What do people do in the summer in Yakutsk?

Explore words in context

4 **Match the words and phrases from the blog with the definitions below.**

> fall   outdoors   indoors   sub-zero conditions   melt   rise

1 inside a house or building
2 outside a house or building
3 get lower
4 change from solid to liquid
5 get higher
6 when the temperature is less than 0 °C

Your turn

5 **Ask and answer with your partner.**

1 How is life in your town different in summer and in winter? In what way?
2 Do you prefer winter or summer? Why?

> In the summer, it's very hot. I prefer the winter because …

6 **Write a short blog entry.**

- Describe the weather in winter and summer in your area.
- Say what you're doing now.

In the winter, it's really cold. The temperatures are below freezing and it snows a lot.

At the moment, I'm writing this blog and I'm watching …

FREEZING IN SIBERIA!

Yakutsk

December 12

It's winter here in Yakutsk. I'm sitting indoors and writing my blog because it's too cold to go outside. It's not snowing now but I'm looking at the thermometer outside and it says –34 °C!

Yakutsk in Russia is the coldest town on Earth. From November to March, it's only light for three or four hours a day and the temperature hardly ever rises above freezing. The average daytime temperature is –30 °C and at night it sometimes falls as low as –60 °C.

Well, I'm not going out today – I'm staying indoors. People don't go out a lot here, at –20 °C, the air freezes inside your nose. At –40 °C, you can't stay outdoors for more than ten minutes. At –45 °C, the metal on your glasses sticks to your face! I'm learning how to play a popular sport called kyyly – a kind of jumping competition. It uses a lot of energy and it keeps you warm and strong. I play kyyly three times a week. I'm trying to keep fit, which is really important when you live in sub-zero conditions!

In summer, Yakutsk is a different city. The snow melts and the temperature rises to 30 °C and more, but people are usually happy to have a heatwave after ten months of winter. It's the season of 'white nights', when it never gets dark, not even at midnight. Camping and barbecues are the favourite summer activities. You can't imagine how much I am looking forward to it!

FACT! *In Yakutsk, Siberia, the lowest ever recorded temperature was –60 °C.*

Language focus 1 Present simple vs. present continuous

1 **Complete the examples from the text on page 10. Then complete the rules in the box.**

1 It's .... now but **I'm looking** at the thermometer outside and **it says** –34 °C!

2 I .... how to play a popular local sport called kyyly. It .... a lot of energy.

We use the present [1] .... to talk about what normally happens, routines and facts. We use the present [2] .... to talk about what is happening now or around now.

3 The temperature .... rises above freezing.

4 It .... falls as low as –60 °C.

5 People are .... happy to have a heatwave after ten months of winter.

We use adverbs and expressions of frequency to explain how often we do things. We use them with the [3] .... Adverbs of frequency go before the verb but after the verb *be*.

➡ **Grammar reference • page 99**

2 🔊 **1.10** **Complete the text with the correct form of the present simple or the present continuous. Use the verbs in brackets. Then listen and check.**

Meg is in Siberia for a year at the university in Yakutsk and life is very different. In the UK, she usually [1] ....*drives*...... (drive) to university. In Yakutsk, she [2] .... (take) the bus every day. She [3] .... (study) Russian in the UK and she'd like to be a translator. She's got exams this week so she [4] .... (study) really hard. She says, 'Right now I [5] .... (read) a book in Russian. I [6] .... (try) not to use the dictionary too much.' She [7] .... (have) a great time in Yakutsk because she [8] .... (go) to the university International Club twice a week. They [9] .... (organise) activities and she meets lots of local students there. 'It's great fun. The people are really nice and I [10] .... (learn) a lot of Russian.'

3 **Add expressions of frequency to make sentences that are true for you.**

1 It's very cold in my town. *It's usually very cold in my town.*

2 I get to school late.

3 My class goes on school trips in June.

4 It's sunny and warm in spring.

5 We go camping.

Your turn

4 **Work with a partner. Discuss the sentences.**

1 Tell your partner about your daily routine.

2 Imagine you're staying in Yakutsk for a month. Tell your partner about how your life is different.

> I usually get up at about 7.30. Then I have breakfast. … Now I'm living in Yakutsk, I get up later …

Learn about someone living in a cold country.

● What does the Kilcher family do during the day?

● What are they preparing for?

● Why did they have to make another plan?

DISCOVERY EDUCATION™

1.1 The long winter

Vocabulary Survival essentials

1 🔊 **1.11** **Match the words with the items in the picture. Then listen, check and repeat.**

> sun cream   water bottle   sunglasses   compass
> map   sleeping bag   penknife   torch
> first aid kit   camera   glasses   contact lenses

2 **Ask and answer with your partner.**
1 Which of the things in Exercise 1 do you have on your mobile phone?
2 Which of the things do you have at home?

➡ **Vocabulary Bank • page 107**

Listening A conversation

3 **Work in small groups. Look at the photo and answer the questions.**
1 What do you think are the dangers of walking in a landscape like this?
2 What do you need to survive for three days there?

4 🔊 **1.12** **Listen to two friends discussing a news story about a hiker. Does it have a happy or sad ending?**

5 🔊 **1.12** **Listen again and answer the questions.**
1 In which country was Sam travelling?
2 What happened to him?
3 What was the weather like?
4 How long was he lost for?
5 What objects did Sam have with him?
6 How did the contact lenses save him?
7 How did they find him in the end?

Your turn

6 **Imagine you are lost in the mountains in the winter. With a partner decide how important the things in Exercise 1 are.**
- Put them in order of importance (1 = very important; 12 = not important).
- Compare your list with another pair.
- Think of three other things that are useful.

A: I think ... is/are important because ...

B: I don't agree. I think ...

Language focus 2 Past simple vs. past continuous

1 Complete the examples from the listening on page 12. Then complete the rules and choose the correct words in the box.

1 One morning he **went** jogging.
2 While he .... **jogging** he got lost.
3 He .... **running** and **listening** to music.
4 He .... **see** where he was going.
5 How long .... he **lost** for?
6 .... someone **looking** for him?

> We use the past ¹.... to talk about finished actions in the past. We use the past ².... to talk about actions in progress in the past.
> ³ We use *when / while* before the past simple.
> ⁴ We use *when / while* before the past continuous.

⊙ **Grammar reference • page 99**

2 Choose the correct verbs to complete the sentences.

1 Sam jogged /(was jogging) when he got / was getting lost.
2 I watched / was watching the news when I saw / was seeing an interesting story.
3 When the helicopter found / was finding him, a lot of people looked / were looking for him.
4 When he ran / was running out of water, he still tried / was still trying to find the ranch.
5 It didn't rain / wasn't raining when Sam started / was starting his run.
6 He lost / was losing his sunglasses while he walked / was walking in the outback.

3 Rewrite the sentences in two different ways. Use *when* or *while*.

1 Peter was walking in the forest. He got lost.
   While Peter was walking in the forest, he got lost.
   Peter was walking in the forest when he got lost.
2 We were driving. A dog ran in front of our car.
3 She was looking at the map. She dropped her camera.
4 I was reading the compass. Julia was putting on suncream.
5 We were sleeping in our tent. It started to rain.

4 🔊 **1.13** Complete the text with the correct form of the verbs in brackets. Then listen and check.

TEENAGERS IN CANYON RESCUE

Emergency services ¹ *rescued* (rescue) two teenagers, Nicholas Ramirez and Kyndall Cendoya, last night after a three-day hunt in Falls Canyon, California. The teenagers ² .... (walk) during the Easter holidays when they ³ .... (disappear) late on Tuesday night. It ⁴ .... (rain) heavily and there were high winds. The teenagers ⁵ .... (not have) any food or water and they ⁶ .... (not carry) any dry clothes in their backpacks. They ⁷ .... (find) a cave and ⁸ .... (stay) there for two nights. On the third day, a local hiker ⁹ .... (see) them. They ¹⁰ .... (sleep) in the cave. A rescue helicopter ¹¹ .... (come) to take them home.

Your turn

5 Write six questions. Use the words from the boxes and the past simple or past continuous.

what when where why	do come sleep watch go eat listen	last night morning yesterday at 8am during the English class

Why were you sleeping during the English class?

6 Ask and answer with your partner.

A: What were you doing yesterday at 8 am?
B: I was watching TV.

Discover Culture

India

1 Work with a partner. Look at the photo of the mangrove jungle. How do you think it is different from a normal jungle?

2 In which one do you think it would be easier to live? Why? Consider transport, food and climate.

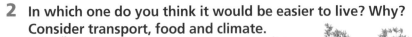

A mangrove jungle

A jungle

Find out about the challenges of living in the mangrove jungle.

DISCOVERY
EDUCATION™

1.2 People of the mangrove jungle

3 ▶ 1.2 Watch the first half of the video (until 1.00). Mark the sentences true (T) or false (F).
1 In India, the River Ganges runs into the sea.
2 There are 1,000 islands in the Sunderbans.
3 One of these islands is called Bali.
4 Life is quite easy there.
5 The people live off rice, fish and potatoes.

4 ▶ 1.2 Watch the second half of the video. Put this information into the correct order.
a They decided to build a high wall to protect their homes.
b They ate the fish.
c They saw the sea level rise.
d They noticed a break in the wall.
e They worked for three hours to fix the break.
f They caught a lot of fish.
g They remembered that their village flooded years ago.

5 ▶ 1.2 Watch the video again. Read Exercises 1 and 2 again. Are your answers the same now? How do the images show the positive and negative side of life in the Mangrove Jungle?

6 Test your memory. These sentences describe different images in the video but each one has a mistake. Correct the false information.
1 There are dry rice fields.
2 There are four men on the boat.
3 We see a half moon.
4 There's a man carrying a lantern on his head.

7 ▶ 1.2 Watch the video again and check your answers.

8 What is life like in the Indian Mangroves? Choose the best summary.
1 Life is okay in the mangroves if you are careful.
2 Life is very hard in the mangroves.
3 Life is easy and relaxed in the mangroves.

Your turn

9 Work with a partner. Is there any part of your country like the Mangroves? Is there an area surrounded by a lot of water? Would you like to live there? Why?/Why not?
There are lots of towns on the river and they are sometimes flooded, so I wouldn't like to live there.

Reading A magazine article

1 Work with a partner. Look at the photo and answer the questions.

1 Where do you think this place is?
2 What do you think is special about it?

2 🔊 1.14 Read the article and check your answers.

3 Read the article again and complete the information.

Approximate distance from the mainland: *4,000 km*
Official language:
Approximate distance from London:
Number of families:
Length of island:
Number of schools:
Month and year that the volcano erupted:

🔍 **Explore** prepositional phrases

4 Find the phrases in the article and complete them using *in* or *on*.

1 *On* Earth 4 .... a ship
2 .... the middle 5 .... total
3 .... the planet 6 .... the island

➡ **Vocabulary Bank** • page 107

Your turn

5 Work with a partner. Compare the life on islands like Bali and Tristan de Cunha. How are they similar?

> They are both islands and they are small communities.

> Something bad happened on both islands – the volcano erupted on Tristan and there was flooding on Bali.

THE REMOTEST INHABITED ISLAND ON EARTH!

Africa

Cape Town

Tristan da Cunha

In the middle of the Atlantic Ocean, more than 4,000 km from the nearest land, is the remotest inhabited island on the planet – it is also a volcanic island. To get there, you need to travel for five or six days on a ship from Cape Town in South Africa.

Tristan da Cunha is a British territory, named after the Portuguese explorer who discovered the island. The official language is English, but London is almost 10,000 km away. The British monarch is the head of state and they use British pounds as their currency.

The island is home to eighty families, about 250 people in total. The island is only 10 km long and there is one town with only one school. This is the only place on the island with an internet connection.

In October 1961, the island's volcano erupted and the whole population went to live in the UK. They got jobs and new homes, but they didn't like the lifestyle there and missed their life on the island. They found it very hard to live in a society where money is the most important thing. So, in November 1962, they returned to Tristan da Cunha – they were happier without television, cars and the stress of modern life!

FACT! *Queen Mary Peak, the volcano in the middle of the island, is 2000 metres high – and it's active!*

Speaking Giving your opinion

Real talk: Which do you prefer – towns and cities or the countryside?

1 ▶ **1.3** Watch the teenagers in the video. How many of them …
a) like the countryside?
b) like towns or cities?
c) like both?

2 💬 Which do *you* prefer – towns and cities or the countryside? Ask and answer with your partner.

3 🔊 **1.15** Listen to Mark and Kate talking about their town. What places do they talk about?

4 Complete the conversation with the useful language.

Useful language

I (don't) think (so) …	Yes, I suppose so.
Maybe, but …	OK, perhaps you're
I reckon …	right, …
I (don't) agree …	

Kate:	Do you live near the school, Mark?
Mark:	No, I live in Chesterton. Do you know it?
Kate:	Yes, I live there too. I ¹......*think*...... it's a great place to live.
Mark:	²… so! Nothing ever happens, and there's nothing to do. It's boring.
Kate:	Well, I don't ³… . There are lots of things to do. What about the sports centre and the youth club?
Mark:	Maybe, ⁴… all my friends live here in town, and I can't go out with them in the evening.
Kate:	OK, ⁵… right – that is a problem, but I ⁶… Chesterton is healthier than town.
Mark:	The air you mean? Yes, ⁷… so. I like taking my dog for walks in the country.
Kate:	You see? Maybe living in a village isn't all bad.
Mark:	OK, perhaps you're ⁸… !

5 🔊 **1.15** Listen again and check your answers.

6 💬 Work with a partner. Practise the conversation in Exercise 4.

7 💬 Work with a partner. Prepare a conversation like the one in Exercise 4. Use the photos below and the useful language. Practise the conversation with your partner.

A Living in a city

B Going to a big school

Writing An email to a friend

1 **Look at the photos and read Artur's email to a pen friend. Where does Artur live?**

New mail +1

Hi,

Thanks for your email. It's great to hear from you!

I live in a small town in the north of Norway, called Tromsø. It's a special place because in summer we have 60 polar days. It never gets dark and we have the midnight sun. I love the summer!

We do a lot of outdoor activities like trekking in the mountains, bike riding, concerts, boating, barbeques on the beach and sunbathing. We need the sun because in the winter we have 60 polar nights when it's always dark! In winter, tourists come here to see the famous northern lights (the aurora borealis). They are amazing!

Where do you live? What do you do there?

Write back soon,

Best wishes,

Artur

2 **Read Artur's email again. Put the information in the correct order.**
- closing the email
- a description of his town
- questions to his friend
- opening the email *1*
- activities he does at different times of the year

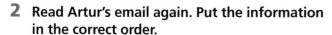 **Useful language**

We use special phrases to open and close an email to a friend:
- Opening an email: *Thanks for your email. …., …. , ….*
- Closing an email: *Write back soon, Best wishes, …. , …. ,*

3 **Look at the Useful language box. Add the examples below to it.**

> How are you (and your family)?
> Thanks for all your news.
> Write back and tell me your news.
> It was great to get your email.
> Hope to hear from you soon.

 Get Writing

PLAN

4 **Plan an email to Artur describing where you live. Use Exercise 2 to help you and make notes.**

WRITE

5 **Write your email. Use your notes from Exercise 4 and the model text to help you.**

CHECK

6 **Can you say YES to these questions?**
- Is the information from Exercise 4 in your email?
- Have you got opening and closing phrases in your email?

A balancing act

Discovery
EDUCATION™

In this unit ...

Get up and go! p21

A life on Broadway p24

What makes a good friend? p26

CLIL Mountain rescue p116

Vocabulary
- Priorities
- Verb + noun collocations
- Performing
- Prepostions of place

Language focus
- *should/must*
- *(don't) have to* vs. *mustn't*

Unit aims
I can ...
- talk about daily routines and priorities.
- understand an article about the importance of sleep.
- understand a radio interview.
- understand an article about special schools.
- offer and accept help.
- write about life at a summer camp.

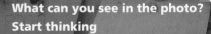
BE CURIOUS

What can you see in the photo?
Start thinking
- Do you write notes like this to remind you?
- What makes you stressed? What makes you happy?
- How does this picture make you feel?

Vocabulary Priorities

1 🔊 **1.16** **Match the phrases with the photos (a–h). Write the letters below. Then listen, check and repeat.**

_c._ do sports

.... shop for clothes

.... hang out with friends

.... do something creative

.... get enough sleep

.... have time for yourself

.... help around the house

.... chat with friends online

2 🔊 **1.17** **Listen to the teenagers. Match the speakers with the activities in Exercise 1.**

1 *have time for yourself*

3 **Think of an adjective or phrase to describe the activities in Exercise 1. Explain your words and phrases to your partner.**

A: I thought of 'boring' for picture a, because I hate shopping for clothes!

B: For picture a, I thought of 'a day out with my friends' because I love going shopping with them.

Your turn

4 **Make notes about the activities in Exercise 1. Then talk to your partner.**

1 Which two things in the list in Exercise 1 are most important to you? Why?

2 Which things do you argue about with your parents?

3 Which one thing stresses you most? Why?

4 Which activities do you have a good time doing?

5 For which activities do you have to be responsible?

I think the most important thing for me is having time for myself – so I can just relax and do what I want to do!

→ **Vocabulary Bank • page 108**

Life is busy with school, hor
sports and other activities an
need to catch up on your slee

Here are three reasons why you should get

YOUR BODY NEEDS SLEEP
As a teenager, you *must* get enough sleep – mc
than an adult. Your body is still growing and your
is still developing. Experts say that you should ge
between eight and nine hours of sleep each night.

SLEEP HELPS YOU DO BETTER AT SCHOOL
When you're tired you can't concentrate in your
lessons. It's more difficult to learn.

SLEEP KEEPS YOU HEALTHY
Without enough sleep, your body gets weak, and
it's easy for you to catch a cold and other illnesses.
When you're tired you often eat food with more sugar
in it and that isn't good for you.

A GOOD NIGHT'S
SLEEP

Did YOU know?

TEENAGERS WHO GET ENOUGH SLEEP ...
- usually have better skin.
- eat less junk food.
- are less likely to experience depression.

Reading A magazine article

1 Work with a partner. Look at the photo and answer the questions.

1 How many hours of sleep do you think teenagers need?

2 What can happen if you don't get enough sleep?

2   1.18 Read the article and check your answers. What's the main aim of the article?

a To offer advice to teenagers.

b To tell teenagers why their parents complain.

3 Read the article again. Answer the questions.

1 Why do teenagers need more sleep than adults?

2 How many hours of sleep do teenagers need every night?

3 What happens at school if you don't get enough sleep?

4 Why do teens eat unhealthy food when they are tired?

5 What two things should you avoid to get a good night's sleep?

Explore verb + noun collocations

4 Find the collocations in the article. Match verbs (1–6) with nouns (a–f) to form collocations.

1	get	a	in your lessons
2	concentrate	b	the Internet
3	catch	c	more sleep
4	watch	d	a snack
5	surf	e	a cold
6	have	f	TV

➡ **Vocabulary Bank • page 108**

Your turn

5 Ask and answer with your partner.

1 What time do you usually go to bed during the week?

2 Do you find it difficult to get to sleep? Why/Why not?

3 Do you like sleeping late at the weekend?

4 Do you think you get enough sleep? What things stop you sleeping?

I usually go to bed at ...

I find it difficult to get to sleep, because ...

I love sleeping late at the weekend! I usually get up at ...

I don't always get enough sleep, because ...

How to get a good night's sleep:

● You shouldn't watch TV, surf the Internet or play computer games before you go to bed. To get to sleep, you need to feel relaxed.

● If you're hungry, have a light snack. You mustn't eat a big meal before you go to bed – it will keep you awake.

● You shouldn't drink any drinks with caffeine or sugar in the evening.

> **FACT!** *Some high schools in the US start classes later so that students can sleep a little longer.*

Language focus 1
should/must

1 Complete the examples from the text on page 20. Then complete the rules in the box.

1 You .... get enough sleep.
2 You .... get between eight and nine hours of sleep each night.
3 You .... watch TV before you go to bed.

We use ¹.... to say what we think is a good idea and ².... to say what we think is necessary.

➔ Grammar reference • page 100

2 Complete the sentences below with *should* or *shouldn't* and the verbs in the box.

say ~~get~~ go to bed spend

1 How many hours of sleep ..*should*.. people ...*get*... every week?
2 Teenagers .... at least an hour a day doing something relaxing.
3 You .... late the night before an important exam.
4 What .... you .... to your parents to convince them that you need more sleep?

3 Complete the sentences with *must* or *mustn't*.

1 You ....*must*.... see the sleep project they uploaded on the school website. It's great!
2 I .... forget to take my project to school tomorrow. I forgot it yesterday and today!
3 What .... parents do to make sure their children are getting enough sleep?
4 You .... come to my party this weekend. I really want you there!

4 🔊 **1.19** Complete the conversation with the correct words. Then listen and check.

A: Are you coming out on Friday?
B: No. My parents have told me I ¹(should)/ shouldn't (it's a good idea) stay in this weekend. I really ² must / mustn't study for that Maths exam. I can't fail another one.
A: Life isn't all about Maths. You ³ must / should hang out with your friends too.
B: Yes, but I'm really tired.
A: Well, you ⁴ should / shouldn't go to bed so late!
B: Yes, but what about the Maths exam?
A: Your parents are right. You ⁵ mustn't / shouldn't fail the next Maths exam and you ⁶ must / should relax before you go to bed.
B: Okay! I really ⁷ must / mustn't get back to my books. I ⁸ should / shouldn't even be talking to you! Good night!

> **Your turn**

5 Think of two problems. Make notes.

I want to get a dog but my parents don't like the idea. What should I do?

I argued with my best friend and now s/he won't speak to me. What should I do?

6 Work with a partner. Talk about your problems and give advice for each situation.

If your parents don't like dogs, you mustn't get one!
You should try to speak to her in a few days' time.

Learn about a new invention.
● What kind of machine are the inventors trying to build?
● What will the machine do?
● What do you think of the machine they build?

Discovery EDUCATION™

2.1 Get up and go!

Listening A radio interview

1 **Work with a partner. Look at the photos and answer the questions.**

   1 What sort of singer do you think she is learning to be?

   2 What do you think she has to learn?

2 🔊 **1.20** **Listen to an interview with Jenny Gregson. Check your answers to the questions in Exercise 1.**

3 🔊 **1.20** **Listen again. Complete the notes.**

My week	
Every day	1 ..... *piano* ..... practice 2 .... exercises 3 ....
Tuesday/Thursday	4 .... lessons 5 study ....
Monday/ Wednesday/Friday	6 .... lessons
Saturday	7 .... classes 8 .... classes

Vocabulary Performing

4 🔊 **1.21** **Complete the sentences with the words in the box. Then listen, check and repeat.**

> orchestra   act   instruments   ~~voice~~
> plays the piano   dancing   on stage   microphone

   1 Have you heard Paul singing? He's got a really powerful ..... *voice* ..... .

   2 When the band played the last song, everybody was .... .

   3 Jenny .... very well. She practises a lot.

   4 We went to the Concert Hall last night. The .... played beautifully.

   5 Nobody could hear her singing because the .... was broken.

   6 When the singer came ...., she looked very nervous.

   7 You play the piano and the guitar. Do you play any other .... ?

   8 Keanu Reeves is very handsome but can he .... ?

➡ **Say it right! • page 96**

Your turn

5 **Ask and answer with your partner.**

   1 Can you sing, dance, act or play an instrument?

   2 Have you ever done any of these activities on stage or in public? How did you feel?

   3 Are you learning to do something new?

> I can play the piano.

> I played the piano at a school concert once. I was very nervous.

> I'm learning to play the guitar. I'm not very good at it!

➡ **Vocabulary Bank • page 108**

Language focus 2 *(don't) have to*

1 Complete the examples from the listening on page 22. Then choose the words to complete the rule.

Present	Past
+ I .... practise every day. She **has to do** voice exercises.	I **had to** sing with a microphone. She **had to** train for many years.
- We .... dance.	I **didn't have to** learn a new song.
? .... you .... take singing lessons? **Does** she **have to** go to piano lessons?	**Did** you **have to** sing that song? **Did** she **have to** learn Italian?

We use *have to* to say what is necessary to do / give someone a choice of what to do.

➡ Grammar reference • page 100

2 🔊 **1.25** Complete the sentences with the correct form of *(don't) have to* and the verbs in the box. Then listen and check.

> practise   make   go (x2)   not take   not go

Dad: Amy, can you come and help me in the kitchen, please?

Amy: Sorry Dad, I ¹ *have to go* somewhere.

Dad: ² .... you .... right now? Can't it wait?

Amy: I promised to go round to Joe's house. He ³ .... for his music exam. He needs me to help him.

Dad: It's just that I ⁴ .... a cake for your grandfather's birthday and I need some help.

Amy: OK then, but please tell Mum I ⁵ .... the dog for a walk this afternoon.

Dad: OK, thanks! The dog ⁶ .... out until this evening. I can take him.

Amy: OK, great!

Your turn

3 Work with a partner. Ask questions using *Do you have to ... ?*

- tidy your room
- get up early at weekends
- practise a musical instrument
- look after your younger brother or sister
- study at the weekend
- wash your parents' car
- train for a sport
- prepare for a show or concert

A: *Do you have to tidy your room?*
B: *Yes, I have to tidy it every week.*

don't have to vs. *mustn't*

4 Look at the example sentences and complete the rules.

- We **don't have to** dance.
- You **mustn't talk** too much.

We use ¹ .... to say it's not necessary to do something.
We use ² .... to say it's important **not** to do something.

➡ Grammar reference • page 100

5 🔊 **1.26** Complete the letter with *don't have to* or *mustn't* and the verbs in the box. Then listen and check.

> dance   bring   speak   wear   forget

Dear Students

The school disco is this Friday at 7 pm. Please remember that you ¹ .... to ask your parents for permission. They ² .... to your teacher (it's not necessary – just sign the form). You ³ .... school uniform but you must wear suitable clothing. Also, you ⁴ .... friends from other schools – they aren't allowed in the school. Finally, don't forget – you ⁵ .... , but it's much more fun if you do!!

Discover Culture

North America

Find out about life on the stage.

Discovery EDUCATION™

▶ 2.2 **A life on Broadway**

1 **Work with a partner. Look at the photos and answer the questions.**

1 In which famous street in New York do they perform musicals and plays?

2 How do you think child actors lives are different to yours? Think about school, social activities, money.

2 ▶ 2.2 **Watch the video and check your answers to question 1.**

3 ▶ 2.2 **Watch the video again. What subjects do they talk about?**

- Being a popular celebrity
- Working long hours
- Living away from home
- Studying for exams
- Earning a lot of money
- Performing for judges

4 ▶ 2.2 **Watch the video again and choose the correct words.**

1 Many kids dream of **being a director / performing** on Broadway.

2 Many children train **full-time / part-time** to be actors and performers.

3 A lot of them leave home **before / when** they are teenagers.

4 **Most / Some** child actors earn a lot of money.

5 The set designer **decides / explains** what goes on stage.

6 The lighting designer helps **invent / create** the world of the play.

7 The best moment for actors is when the audience **claps / laughs**.

5 **Test your memory. Are the sentences true or false? Correct the false ones.**

1 Annie has blond hair and blue eyes.

2 Her dog is big and light brown.

3 The girls are cleaning the floor with a brush and a bucket of water.

4 The special effects include rain and snow.

6 ▶ 2.2 **Watch the video again and check your answers.**

Your turn

7 **Discuss the questions with your partner.**

1 Which do you think are advantages and disadvantages of being a child actor?

2 Are there any theatre schools near where you live?

3 Would you like to attend a theatre school? Why/Why not?

Reading An article

1 Work with a partner. Look at the photos. Why do you think boys and girls want to go to these schools?

2 🔊 **1.27** Read about the football academy La Masia and the Royal Ballet School. Find three ways in which the schools are similar.

3 Read the article again. Which school do the sentences describe? Write LM (La Masia), RB (Royal Ballet) or B (both).

1 The school only has boys. *LM*
2 Students have normal school and training.
3 They have time off in the evenings.
4 The school also has international students.
5 They have a rest in the afternoon.
6 To get into the school, they have to show how good they are.

Explore prepositions

4 Look at the highlighted words in the text. Complete the sentences with the words in the box.

> of   in front of   between   near   until   over

1 At our school concerts, we sing .... our parents and friends.
2 There are .... 10 international students in my class.
3 My class is full .... really talented dancers.
4 We have lessons .... two o'clock and then we practise dancing.
5 The school isn't .... to where many children live, so they live with other families.
6 The school is for boys and girls .... the ages of 11 and 16.

➡ **Vocabulary Bank • page 108**

Your turn

5 Ask and answer with your partner.
1 Are there any schools like these in your country?
2 Would you like to go to a school like these ones? Why?/Why not?
3 Would you like to live away from home?
4 What would you miss most?

I think there are football academies in my country.

6 Write about a time when you won or when you were successful at something. How did you feel?

I remember once ...
I felt great because ...

La Masia Football Academy, BARCELONA

La Masia is Barcelona's football academy. Some of the greatest footballers in the world have come from La Masia. The World Cup and the European Championships were full **of** players from this academy. There are about 80 boys **between** the ages of 11 and 18 at the academy. They go to school **until** half past two in the afternoon, then they have lunch and a siesta. Most boys have to use this time to study and do their homework. In the evening, they watch TV or play video games before they go to bed. For these boys, football is their life. They train hard because they want to be the best.

FACT! *The amount of energy needed to perform a ballet is about the same as playing two full football matches or running almost 29 kilometres.*

The Royal Ballet School, LONDON

The Royal Ballet School in the heart of London trains dancers and choreographers. The school has two buildings, one **near** Richmond Park for 11 to 16-year-olds and the other in Covent Garden for older students. Students at the school mix normal school subjects with their dance classes. Many famous ballet dancers have come from this school. To get into the school, students have to audition – they have to perform **in front of** judges from the school. **Over** 2,000 children attended auditions for the school in 2012. About 70 boys and girls get a place each year. There are students from all over the world. In the evening, when students aren't in class or practising ballet, they can play tennis or play table football in the student halls.

💬 Speaking Offering to help

Real talk: What makes a good friend?

1 ▶ **2.3** Watch the teenagers in the video. What activities do you hear? What do you think makes a good friend?

- helps with decisions
- likes to talk on the phone
- thinks of other people and is helpful
- buys good birthday presents
- has to just be there
- is honest
- likes to go out on the weekend
- helps with homework
- listens
- does all the same activities

2 💬 What do *you* think makes a good friend?

3 🔊 **1.28** Laura is talking to Olivia, a new student at her school. What does Laura offer to do?

4 Complete the conversation with the useful language.

Useful language

Offering to help	Asking for help
Here, let me show you.	I'm not sure how to …
What do you need?	Can I ask you something?
I'll give you a hand.	
All you have to do is …	

Olivia: Hey, Laura. Can I ¹ ....*ask you*.... something?
Laura: Yeah, sure. What's up?
Olivia: It's this Science project. I'm ² .... to organise it.
Laura: Mr Brown's put instructions on the school Intranet. What do ³ .... ?
Olivia: Well, how do I get access to the Intranet?
Laura: You have to type in your password. Here, let ⁴ .... you.
Olivia: Thanks. That's really nice of you!
Laura: It's simple. All you have ⁵ .... is follow the instructions and format it correctly.
Olivia: Oh no! I'm not very good at things like that.
Laura: Don't worry. I'll ⁶ .... a hand if you like.
Olivia: Great! Thanks a lot.

5 🔊 **1.28** Listen again and check your answers.

6 💬 Work with a partner. Practise the conversation in Exercise 4.

7 💬 Work with a partner. Prepare a conversation like the one in Exercise 4. Use the useful language and your own ideas. Practise the conversation with your partner.

Situation 1

You want to download a video but you don't know how.

Student A Explain the problem.

Student B Help Student A. Give him/her ideas about how to find the video, save or download it and where to save it.

Situation 2

You can't find any material for a school project.

Student B Explain the problem.

Student A Help Student B Give him/her help on where to find ideas, i.e. the Internet, the library or interviewing people.

✎ Writing A competition entry

1 Look at the photos and read Jon's competition entry. What were his favourite things about summer camp?

WIN A FREE WEEK AT OUR SUMMER CAMP!
Did you go to summer camp? Tell us about your stay. We publish the best ones on our website!

I didn't want to go to summer camp. I imagined an awful place with lots of rules, so Beaufort Camp was a big surprise. We didn't have to get up early and there was plenty of time for breakfast before we started activities at 10 o'clock. There were lots to choose from and they were fun. My favourites were canoeing, volleyball and horse riding. At night, we sat round a fire and we could even sleep outside if we wanted to! The weather was boiling but there was a big swimming pool to cool us down. For me, camp was an incredible experience. I made lots of friends. You should try it!

JONZ

2 Look back at Jon's competition entry again. What does Jon write about?

- favourite activities (daytime / at night)
- the monitors / other campers
- the daily routine
- why he liked it
- the food
- the weather

Useful language

Avoiding repetition (1)
We can use reference words so that we don't repeat the same word.
*We started activities at 10 o'clock. There were **lots** (of activities) to choose from, and **they** (these activities) were fun.*

3 Look at the Useful language box. Find one other way of avoiding repetition of the word *activities* in the text in Exercise 1.

4 Change the phrases in bold in the text so you don't repeat the words.
The best thing about wild camping was the *animals*. There were lots of ¹ **animals** if you looked carefully. On the second day, I saw some *falcons*. ² **The falcons** flew over the trees near the campsite. But the most active animals were *the goats*. ³ **The goats** jump up and down the mountains incredibly fast! I was also amazed at ⁴ **the goats'** huge horns.

✎ Get writing

PLAN

5 Plan your competition entry for the camp website. Include information from Exercise 2 to help you. Decide what order you are going to put them in.

WRITE

6 Write your competition entry for the camp website. Use your notes from Exercise 5 and the model text to help you.

CHECK

7 Can you say YES to these questions?
- Is the information from Exercise 2 in your email?
- Have you avoided a lot of repetition?

Vocabulary

1 Write the extreme weather words for each picture.

1 *boiling*

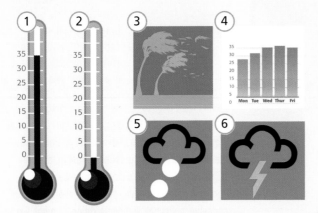

2 Complete the sentences with the words in the box. There are two extra words.

> sleeping bag   camera   first aid kit
> penknife   ~~sun cream~~   compass   torch

1 You need *sun cream* to protect your skin against sunburn.

2 You need a .... to find your way in the dark.

3 You need a warm .... if you're camping.

4 You need a .... to find the correct direction.

5 You need a .... in case you get hurt.

3 Complete the sentences with the correct form of the phrases in the box.

> help around the house   get enough sleep
> hang out with friends   do something creative
> ~~shop for clothes~~   chat with friends online
> do sports   have time for yourself

1 I don't like *shopping for clothes* . I'm not really interested in fashion.

2 I need to be alone sometimes. I like .... myself.

3 I hate ..... Housework is so boring!

4 I .... to stay in touch with them.

5 I dream about ..... I only usually get about 6 hours a night.

6 I want to be a designer or an artist. I'm really happy when I'm .....

7 I play football for a club and I love swimming. We also .... at school.

8 When I'm not doing homework or with my family I like to .... .

4 Choose the correct words.

1 Lea sings beautifully. She's got a lovely (voice)/ microphone.

2 I play the violin in the school **instrument / orchestra**.

3 Pete is learning his lines – he's **dancing / acting** in the end of term play.

4 Do you play **an instrument / the piano**? Yes, I play the **piano / instrument**.

5 Our headteacher uses **a microphone / an instrument** to talk to us in the hall.

6 Are you nervous before you go **acting / on stage**?

Explore vocabulary

5 Choose the correct words.

> **Q:** I'm tired during the day – how can I wake up?!
>
> **A:** [1] **Catch /** (Get) more sleep. Most people need [2] **over / above** six hours sleep a night. Don't sit in front of the TV or [3] **surf / watch** the Internet before you go to bed.
>
> To help you [4] **get more / concentrate** in lessons, spend time [5] **outdoors / indoors** in [6] **front of / between** lessons and get some fresh air. Also, [7] **surf / have** a light snack.
>
> Have the windows open in your classroom and sit [8] **beside / over** the window. When you are [9] **indoors / outdoors** all day it makes you feel sleepy.

6 Complete the text with the words in the box.

> in   sub-zero conditions   on (x2)   rises
> falls   catch   of

When should I travel to New Zealand?

You may think that New Zealand is one of the warmest places [1] *on* the planet, but New Zealand is full [2] .... surprises! In summer, the temperature [3] .... to an average maximum temperature of between 20 and 30°C, but the temperature [4] .... as you travel south. While the far north has subtropical weather during summer, inland alpine areas of South Island can experience [5] .... as low as -10°C in winter. So wrap up warm if you don't want to [6] .... a cold! One year the people [7] .... the island experienced 40cm of snow [8] .... total in one night.

Language focus

1 **Complete the sentences with the present continuous or present simple of the verbs in the box.**

> read   do   not stay   rain   get   ~~study~~   stay

1 We _are studying_ Japanese at school this term.
2 .... they .... a test right now?
3 They .... up late if they have school the next day.
4 It's nearly the end of September and the weather .... colder.
5 What book .... you .... at the moment?
6 I prefer to .... indoors when it's cold
7 It hardly ever .... in the winter.
8 You look tired. .... you .... enough sleep?

2 **Complete the sentences and questions with the verbs in brackets. Use the past continuous or past simple.**

1 I _saw_ (see) sharks when I _was swimming_ (swim) in the ocean.
2 Jake .... (climb) in the mountains when he .... (drop) his camera.
3 They .... (walk) in the desert when they .... (find) a huge cave.
4 What .... you .... (do) when I .... (phone) you yesterday?
5 It .... (not rain) when we .... (start) hiking.
6 Where .... you .... (jog) when you .... (lose) your mobile?

3 **Complete the sentences with the words in the box.**

> should try   ~~mustn't tell~~   shouldn't stay up
> must finish   should/get   mustn't be

1 You _mustn't tell_ people your password when you surf the Internet.
2 Anna .... to concentrate more in lessons.
3 We .... this school project before Friday.
4 When you chat online you .... unkind to friends.
5 They .... so late doing their homework.
6 How many hours' sleep .... people .... in your opinion?

4 **Choose the correct word.**

1 You **(don't have to)** / **mustn't** practise every day.
2 They **don't have to** / **mustn't** chat to strangers on the Internet.
3 We **don't have to** / **mustn't** sing that song – we can choose a different one.
4 **Do you have to** / **Must you** tidy your room at the weekends?

Language builder

5 **Choose the correct words to complete the conversation.**

> **Sylvia:** Hi, Kylie! ¹ _b_ your homework?
> **Kylie:** No, I ² .... at my photos from my holiday.
> **Sylvia:** I ³ .... that too. ⁴ .... have fun on your holiday?
> **Kylie:** Yes! We ⁵ .... to the mountains. One day, while we ⁶ ...., some wild deer ⁷ .... up to us to find food.
> **Sylvia:** Amazing! I want to go hiking next summer holiday. What ⁸ .... take with me?
> **Kylie:** Well you ⁹ .... take anything too heavy. You ¹⁰ .... take a map because that's on your smartphone. But you ¹¹ .... watch out for snakes.
> **Sylvia:** Snakes? I don't like snakes!

1 a Do you do   b Are you doing   c Do you doing
2 a am look   b looking   c am looking
3 a usually do   b do usually   c am usually doing
4 a You did   b Did you   c Were you
5 a went   b go   c were going
6 a hiked   b were hiking   c hike
7 a come   b were coming   c came
8 a I should   b should I   c do I should
9 a should   b must   c shouldn't
10 a have to   b don't have to   c should
11 a must   b shouldn't   c don't have to

Speaking

6 **Match the sentences.**

1 I'll give you a hand.   _e_
2 I think this city is a great place to live!
3 Can I ask you something?
4 Maybe living in a village isn't all bad.
5 I'm not sure how to use this computer.
6 I reckon that this town is really boring.

a Let me show you.
b OK, perhaps you're right.
c I agree. There are lots of things to do here.
d I disagree. There are lots of things to do here.
e That's really kind.
f Yeah, sure. What's up?

3 Art all around us

In this unit ...

The art of
storytelling **p33**

A world of
music **p36**

Have you ever been
to a concert? **p38**

CLIL Perspective **p117**

Vocabulary
- Art around us
- Collocations
- Musical instruments
- Phrasal verbs with *up*

Language focus
- Present perfect for
  indefinite past time
- Present perfect with
  ever/never

Unit aims
I can ...
- identify different types of art.
- talk about what I have and haven't done.
- ask and answer questions about music.
- understand an article about a festival in
  another country.
- invite a friend somewhere and arrange
  to meet.
- write an Internet post about a concert.

BE CURIOUS

What can you see in the photo?
Start thinking
- **Do you like the mural on
  this building?**
- **Why do think someone
  painted this?**
- **Would you like to live
  in a building like this?**

Vocabulary Art around us

1 🔊 **1.29** Match the words in the box with the art around us (a–j). Which word describes where we see paintings? Then listen, check and repeat.

> concert hall ~~busker~~ living statue juggler sculpture mural
> exhibition gallery painting graffiti portrait painter

a *busker*

2 Complete the chart with the words from Exercise 1.

works of art	places to see art or music	a performer or an artist
		busker

3 🔊 **1.30** Listen to two groups on a day trip in London. What did each group see? Write the words from Exercise 1 in your notebook.
Group 1: *gallery*
Group 2:

Your turn

4 Ask and answer with your partner.

1 Which of the people, places and things in Exercise 1 can you find near where you live?
2 Do you like watching street performers like jugglers and human statues? Why?/Why not?
There's a gallery of modern art quite near my house, but I don't go there very often!

> 👁 **Get it right!**
>
> When we use *there* after *go*, we don't use the preposition *to*.
> *We go **there** three times a week.*
> *Did you go **there** on your own?*

➡ **Vocabulary Bank • page 109**

Reading An online debate

1 Work with a partner. Look at the pictures below. What do you think makes a person an artist?

2 🔊 **1.31** Read the debate. What do Josh and Kirsten think art is?

3 Read the article again. Are these sentences true or false? Correct the false sentences.

1 Josh likes doing graffiti. *F*
2 To Josh, photographs that people post online aren't examples of art.
3 Josh and his friends like the portraits he draws and the photos he takes.
4 Kirsten enjoys going to art museums.
5 Kirsten believes that art is anything that is creative and fun.
6 Kirsten thinks that good art is easy.

Explore collocations

4 Find the collocations in the text. Match the words in box A with the words in box B. Then complete the sentences.

A
> post ~~good~~ passionate take work make

B
> ~~at~~ hard online photos about money

1 I love painting, but I'm not very ...*good at*... it – some of my pictures are terrible!
2 You have to .... to be a good artist.
3 Is it okay to .... these photos of you .... ?
4 My sister loves to .... of unusual buildings.
5 It's very difficult to .... from painting pictures.
6 My sister's really .... juggling. She practises for hours every day.

➡ **Vocabulary Bank • page 109**

Your turn

5 Work in small groups. Have a debate. Is everyone an artist?

- Make notes of different examples to support your opinion.
- Discuss your ideas using your notes.
- Which group made the best argument?

I agree, I think graffiti is …
I'm not sure, I think it depends on …
There are some great examples of graffiti on …

ARTICLES   CONTACT

EVERYONE'S AN

YOU'VE TAKEN A PHOTO AND PUT IT ON A SOCIAL NETWORK SITE. FIFTEEN FRIENDS HAVE GIVEN YOU A 'LIKE'. YOU'RE AN ARTIST!

THE CASE **FOR**:

We look at the *Mona Lisa* or a Picasso painting and we say, 'That's art.' But what about the amazing graffiti someone has painted on your street? What about the poster presentation you've done? You've worked hard and it's great. So, have you made a work of art? To me, art is anything that's creative. Of course, I like going to famous museums but I also like drawing portraits of my friends or taking photos. I'm not very good at these things, but I'm creative. I'm passionate about them, and my friends like them. Most of all, I like them!

Josh, age 15, San Diego, California

THE CASE **AGAINST**:

I have always loved visiting art museums. Why? Because I like looking at good art. Art is not a drawing that a four-year-old child has done, it isn't painting your body crazy colours and standing in the street, and it certainly isn't graffiti. Some people say, 'If it's creative, it's art.' I don't agree. My aunt is an artist. She went to art school, and she has worked in her studio for years. She hasn't made much money, but her sculptures have been in a few exhibitions. Her art is great. You haven't made a work of art if you haven't studied for years and developed your talent.

Kirsten, age 16, Berlin, Germany

WHAT IS *art*?
WHAT'S YOUR OPINION?

FACT! *The British graffiti artist Banksy sold a piece of graffiti for $1.8 million.*

Language focus 1 Present perfect for indefinite past time

1 Complete the examples from the text on page 32. Then choose the words to complete the rule.

1 You _'ve taken_ a photo.
2 What about the poster presentation you .... ?
3 .... you .... a work of art?
4 I .... always .... visiting art museums.
5 She .... much money.
6 You .... a work of art if you haven't studied.

We use the present perfect to talk about events in the past when the time **is / is not** important.

➡ Grammar reference • page 101

⊙ Get it right!

gone and been

gone = to go and not come back
been = to go and come back.
He's gone out. (He's not here now.)
He's been out. (He's back now.)

2 Complete the sentences with an irregular verb from the box. Use the present perfect.

> take   not visit   ~~see~~   meet   go (x2)   play   speak

1 My sister _has seen_ that exhibition three times. She loves it!
2 My grandparents .... to museums all over the world.
3 We .... about ten photos so far.
4 I .... never .... to anyone in English outside class.
5 I .... never .... a famous artist. Have you?
6 He .... to the gallery. He'll be back later.
7 I .... an interesting gallery – they are all very boring!
8 I .... the guitar in three bands.

3 🔊 **1.32** Complete the text with the verbs in brackets. Use the present perfect. Then listen and check.

The Berlin Wall separated East and West Berlin. On the West side, there was lots of political graffiti. Now, some artists ¹_have started_ (start) to recreate the original art. One artist, Bill Neumann explains, 'Well, the idea is very simple. I ² .... (look) at old photos and I ³ .... (make) copies of the graffiti. Other artists ⁴ .... (do) the same thing. We ⁵ .... (recreate) a section of the original wall. It ⁶ .... (be) a really interesting experience for us. We ⁷ .... (not finish) the work, but we hope to soon.'

Your turn

4 Write questions using the prompts.

- see / a busker
- paint / a portrait
- take / a photo of someone famous
- see / good graffiti
- go / concert hall
- post / a photo online
- go / an exhibition

Have you ever seen a busker?

5 Ask and answer with your partner.

> Have you ever seen a busker?

> Yes, I have. I've seen a lot of them in town. Some of them are very good.

Learn about Aboriginal art.
- What do Australian Aboriginals use art for?
- Why are some paintings like 'survival maps'?
- What is a common feature of Aboriginal art?

Discovery EDUCATION™

3.1 The art of storytelling

Vocabulary Instruments

1 🔊 1.33 Match the words in the box with the instruments in the pictures (1–14). Then listen, check and repeat.

> guitar   drums   banjo   flute   violin   saxophone
> keyboards   mouth organ   tambourine   piano
> recorder   trumpet   cello   clarinet

2 Work with a partner. Answer the questions.

1 What instruments do you associate with orchestras and classical music?
2 What instruments do you expect to see in a pop or rock band?
3 What about the other instruments: where would you normally see them?

➡ **Vocabulary Bank • page 109**

Listening An interview

3 Look at the picture of a musician called Leo. What instruments has he got? Where do you think he performs?

4 🔊 1.34 Listen to a journalist, Marcia, interviewing Leo. Check your ideas from Exercise 3.

5 🔊 1.34 Listen again and answer the questions.

1 Where is Marcia?
2 Why is Leo so well known in Auckland?
3 Which of Leo's instruments is new?
4 How long has he played today?
5 What types of music does he play?
6 Which instruments has he never played?

Your turn

6 Work in groups. Do a music survey. Report your group's information to the class.

- Do you like listening to music?
- What kind of music do you like?
- Do you play a musical instrument?
- Do you ever give money to buskers?

People listen to different kinds of music but … .
Some people listen to music on the bus and … .
Two people always give money to buskers because … .

Language focus 2 Present perfect with *ever/never*

1 Complete the examples from the listening on page 34.

1 He's ....*never*.... played here at the festival.
2 Have you .... played at this festival?
3 I've .... played here before.
4 Have you .... played in a group?
5 I've .... played the cello or the violin.

➔ **Grammar reference • page 101**

2 Look at the questions in Exercise 1. Where does *ever* go in the question?

3 Rewrite the questions putting *ever* in the right position.

1 Have you met a famous musician?
2 Have you visited England?
3 Has your town had a music festival?
4 Have your parents owned a pet?

➔ **Say it right! • page 96**

4 Make sentences. For pictures 1–3, write sentences using *never*. For pictures 4–6, write questions using *ever*. Ask and answer with your partner.

1 I / paint / graffiti on a wall

2 he / play / the drums

3 she / win / a race

4 climb / top of a mountain

5 go / a concert

6 paint / a house

5 🔊 **1.37** Write questions using the verbs in brackets. Then listen and check.

The MUSIC QUIZ

1 you (be) to a concert or festival?
2 you (download) music from the Internet?
3 you (be) in a band?
4 you (sing) in a choir?
5 you (upload) a piece of music to the Internet?
6 you (meet) a famous musician or singer?
7 you (travel) a long way to see a group or singer?
8 you (listen) to music while doing sport at the same time?
9 you (post) a music video online?
10 you (follow) a band on Twitter?

Your turn

6 Ask and answer the quiz questions in Exercise 5 with your partner.

Have you ever been to a concert or festival?

No, I've never been to a concert but I've been to a festival.

Discover Culture

Australia

India

Mexico

a

b

c

1 Look at the images of three musical instruments (a–c) and complete the table with information below.

Mexico India Australia ~~sitar~~
didgeridoo trumpet string wind (x2)

	Country	Name of instrument	Type of instrument
Photo A			
Photo B		*sitar*	
Photo C			

Find out about unusual instruments.

DISCOVERY EDUCATION™ ▶

3.2 A world of music

2 ▶ 3.2 Watch the video and check your answers.

3 Match the information to the three different musical traditions or instruments.

Mariachi didgeridoo sitar

1 The music is lively and emotional.
2 The instrument has been around for hundreds of years.
3 A famous group used this instrument and musical style in their own music.
4 This music requires a number of different instruments.
5 This is one of the oldest instruments in the world.
6 More Australians play this instrument now.

4 Test your memory. Mark the sentences true or false. Correct the false ones.

1 We see the Mariachi perform live and when they are practising.
2 There are drums, guitars, violins and trumpets in a Mariachi group.
3 The sitar player closes his eyes when he plays.
4 The Australian Aborigine is sitting with three other people.

5 ▶ 3.2 Watch the video again and check your answers.

6 What is the report's main message? Choose the best option.

1 Every country has different musical traditions.
2 We can now share and listen to different musical styles very easily.
3 Music can be happy or sad, choose the music according to your mood.

Your turn

7 Ask and answer in groups.

1 Would you like to play one of these instruments?
2 Are there any traditional instruments which are special to your country?
3 What do you think are the positive things about playing in a band or orchestra with other people?

Reading A web page

1 Work with a partner. Look at the pictures of a festival in the U.S.A. What do you think people do there?

2 🔊 1.38 Read the text and check your answers to Exercise 1.

3 Read the Frequently Asked Questions (FAQs) about The Burning Man Festival. Match the questions (A–F) to the answers (1–6).

A What else do people do at the festival?
B Has the festival always taken place there?
C What happens after the festival?
D What is The Burning Man Festival?
E How is it different from other festivals?
F Why is it called The Burning Man Festival?

Explore phrasal verbs with *up*

4 Look at the highlighted words in the text. Complete the sentences with the correct form of the words in the box.

show set ~~tidy~~ pick light dress

1 When the festival was over, we ...*tidied*... up all our rubbish and went home.
2 For the festival last year, my friend .... up as a robot.
3 Hundreds of fireworks .... up the sky to end the festival.
4 We asked him to come at eight o'clock but he didn't .... up until nine o'clock.
5 The band .... up their equipment on the stage before the concert.
6 We .... up some food in the supermarket and drove out to the festival site.

➔ **Vocabulary Bank • page 109**

Your turn

5 Ask and answer with your partner.
1 Would you like to go to a festival like The Burning Man? Why?/Why not?
2 Does your school or town have its own festival? What type of festival is it? What can you do there?

> I'd really like to go because it looks amazing in the photos.

6 Write about the last festival you went to.
The last festival I went to was in our town. There were …

Burning Man Festival FAQs

Maybe you've **picked up** tickets to the Festival, but you're not sure what to expect. Read these FAQs to find out more:

1 D.
It's an arts community festival which takes place every year for a week at the end of August in The Black Rock Desert in Nevada, in the U.S.A. More than 60,000 people **showed up** last year. Volunteers create a community in the desert called Black Rock City – they **set up** everything themselves.

2 ...
No, it started in San Francisco, California in 1986, next to the Golden Gate Bridge. It moved to the desert five years later.

3 ...
Because fire is an important theme of the festival. People build an enormous wooden statue of a person which is more than 30 metres tall and they burn it on the Saturday night of the festival. They also build and burn lots of other things.

4 ...
They **dress up** in costumes and because of the dust in the desert they wear goggles. There are also a lot of other fun activities. There is usually a balloon chain of 450 different balloons which is one kilometre long and it **lights up** the sky.

5 ...
After the festival, the rules are very strict: people must **tidy up** everything and leave the desert exactly as it was before the festival started because the organisers are very worried about protecting the environment.

6 ...
It's unusual because there aren't any famous bands or celebrities. It's all about community – everyone is on the same level.

> **FACT!** *Every August, Black Rock City becomes the third largest city in Nevada – but then it disappears in September!*

37

Speaking Invitations and arrangements

Real talk: Have you ever been to a concert?

1 **Watch the teenagers in the video. How many of the teenagers …**

a) have been to more than one concert?
b) prefer to do something else?
c) have played in a concert?

2 💬 Have *you* ever been to a concert?

3 🔊 **1.39 Fran and Nicky are talking. What are they arranging to do?**

4 **Complete the conversation with the useful language.**

5 🔊 **1.39 Listen again and check your answers.**

6 💬 **Work with a partner. Practise the conversation in Exercise 4.**

7 💬 **Change the words in bold in the conversation. Use the ideas below. Take turns to ask and answer the questions.**

Concert 1
The Black Roots
The Hacienda Club
Station Road

Doors open: 9pm   **Band starts:** 9.30

Concert 2
Live concert with
Don't be Shy
The Black Bee Club,
Miller Street

Doors open: 7.30pm   **Band:** 8pm

Useful language

What time shall we meet (then)?	That's a great idea! Let's go together.
Yeah, why not?	How about -*ing* … ?
Do you fancy -*ing* … ?	Shall I (ask my dad to get us)?
Sounds good!	

Fran: Nicky, do you ¹ *fancy going* to a concert tomorrow?

Nicky: Yeah, ² …. ? Who's playing?

Fran: A **pop rock** band called **The Sweets**. They're a new band. I've got free tickets.

Nicky: ³ …. good! Where are they playing?

Fran: The **Apollo Club**, in **Market Street**.

Nicky: OK. What time ⁴ …. meet then?

Fran: It starts at **8.30**, I think. ⁵ …. together. ⁶ …. coming to my house at **half seven**?

Nick: OK. ⁷ …. ask **my dad** to come and get us at the end?

Frank: Yes, that's a ⁸ …. !

Nick: OK. See you tomorrow, then.

✏ Writing An internet post

1 Look at the photos and read Alba's blog about a concert. Did she enjoy it?

I've just come back from a fantastic free concert. It was in a park near the city centre and there was a great atmosphere, with hundreds of young people dancing and enjoying themselves. There were lots of bands but for me the best one was The Hurricane from Manchester. They play a mixture of styles. Their first songs were folk and blues but the last ones sounded more like reggae and rock. The singer (Janie Smith) has a really amazing voice, and the guitarists and drummer played together really well. They've just made an album (they've never had a hit) and I want to get it!!! If you get the chance to see them, go for it ☺!

2 Read Alba's description of the concert. Answer the questions.

Does Alba …
1 say where the concert took place?
2 describe the atmosphere?
3 describe the stage?
4 say who played and give information about the band?
5 say what she had to eat or drink at the concert?
6 give her opinion?
7 make a recommendation?
8 say how much it cost?

Useful language

Avoiding repetition (2)
We use *one* (singular) and *ones* (plural) to refer to something we mentioned earlier in a text.
• *There were lots of bands but for me the best* **one** *was The Hurricane from Manchester.*
• *Their first songs were folk and blues but the last* **ones** *sounded more like reggae and rock.*

3 Look at the Useful language box. What kind of words do *one* and *ones* replace?

4 Complete the sentences with *one* or *ones*.
1 I really liked the last band. The first ......*ones*...... weren't as good.
2 There are two boys in the band. The tall .... plays the drums.
3 They sang two songs. Which .... did you like best?
4 I've seen them in concert twice. The last .... was in the park last summer.
5 I like all their songs but the earlier .... are great to dance to.
6 Dave's got three guitars: a red .... and two black ..... .

 **Get writing**

PLAN

5 Plan a blog post about a concert you've been to. Use Exercise 2 to help you. Decide what order to put them in.

WRITE

6 Write your blog post about the concert. Use your notes from Exercise 5 and the model text to help you.

CHECK

7 Can you say YES to these questions?
• Is the information from the list in Exercise 2 in your writing?
• Have you avoided using repetition?

4 Adventure

Discovery
EDUCATION™

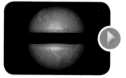
Vocabulary
- Expressions with *go*
- Words from the text
- Phrasal verbs
- Interesting adjectives

Language focus
- Present perfect with *still*, *yet*, *already* and *just*
- Present perfect with *for* and *since*
- Present perfect and past simple

Unit aims
I can ...
- talk about activities.
- understand an online information advertisement about a charity adventure holiday.
- understand a radio interview with teenagers on a school trip.
- understand about culture and customs in New Zealand.
- ask for and understand information about an adventure activity.
- write a travel blog.

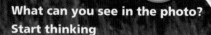

BE CURIOUS

What can you see in the photo?
Start thinking
- What are the men doing?
- What kind of holiday is it?
- What activities do you think they will do?

Vocabulary Expressions with *go*

1 🔊 **1.40** Match the phrases in the box with the photos (a–i). Then listen, check and repeat.

> climbing   a theme park   summer camp   a~~ school exchange~~
> a guided tour   a safari   skiing   sailing   trekking

a   *a school exchange*

2 🔊 **1.41** Listen to the conversation between Chloe and Ben. Where did they go last summer?

3 🔊 **1.41** Listen again and complete the chart with the words in Exercise 1.

go	go on	go to
		a summer camp

4 Look again at the expressions in Exercise 1 and think about the trips. On which trips do you usually a) do an activity? b) sleep away from home? c) use some kind of transport?

You do an activity when you go climbing.
You sleep away from home when you go to a summer camp.

Your turn

5 You and your partner went on a summer camp last year. Choose four activities that you did at the camp from Exercise 1. Ask and answer questions to find out which activities your partner did.

> Did you go climbing?

> Yes, I did. / No I didn't.

➡ **Vocabulary Bank • page 110**

Reading An online advertisement

1 Look at the photos. What are the teenagers doing on the boat? What kind of trip is it?

2 🔊 1.42 Read the online advertisement and check your answers.

3 Read the advertisement again. What does each of the numbers in the box refer to?

> two or three hundred   thousands   30   70 (x2)   40   15   200

Explore words in context

4 Match these words and phrases from the advertisement with the definitions below.

> an exact copy   a taste of   disabled   take it in turns
> keep watch   adjusted   cool stuff

1 stay awake and look out for danger
2 a short experience of something different
3 a very good imitation
4 exciting things to do
5 share the work with other people
6 a condition that makes it difficult to do things most people can do
7 change the way you behave or think

Your turn

5 Ask and answer with your partner. Describe a time when you did something for the first time.
- Where were you?
- What did you do for the first time?
- How did you feel?

> I remember the first time I went skiing … It was really cool!

6 Write a paragraph beginning *I remember the first time I … .*

> *I remember the first time I went sailing. It was a beautiful day but I was very nervous because I didn't know how to swim! …*

LIFE ON THE WAVES

'I've never sailed before. This is my first time and it's an amazing feeling.' Sandra, 16, is on The Stavros S Niarchos, a 200 ft (70 metre) sailing ship, with 40 other young sailors. The Stavros is an exact copy of the ships that pirates sailed two or three hundred years ago. It belongs to the Tall Ships Youth Trust. The Trust offers sailing trips for teenagers and young adults. Every year, thousands of young people get their first taste of the sea. Up to 70% of them are disabled or disadvantaged. For everyone, it's a once in a lifetime experience!

Sandra is on a trip from the Azores, in the North Atlantic, to Spain. The trip lasts a week and they have already been at sea for three days. 'We do everything,' she explained. 'We take the wheel, we cook, we clean and we take it in turns to keep watch at night. I never knew there was so much work on a ship!'

Her friend, Emma, 15, has never been on a boat before either. 'I still haven't adjusted to life at sea.' 'We've done some cool stuff,' says James, 17. 'I've just climbed up and down the mast. It's 30 metres tall and the views are

Language focus 1 Present perfect
with *still, yet, already* and *just*

1 Complete the examples from the text on page 42.

+	They .... **already** .... at sea for three days. I .... **just** .... up and down the mast.
-	I **still** .... to life at sea. We .... any whales **yet**.
?	**Have** you **seen** any dolphins **yet**? How long **have** you **been** at sea?

➡ **Grammar reference** • page 102

2 Look at the chart and complete the sentences using *still, yet, already* and *just*.

1 I'm sorry but the ship has .... *already* .... left. It left about an hour ago.
2 I .... haven't seen any dolphins and we've been on this boat all morning.
3 Has the boat left the port .... ?
4 We've .... come back from a week at sea. It was amazing!
5 The passengers .... haven't got on the ship.
6 We haven't done any training .... . We're starting this afternoon.
7 Don't go into the ship's kitchen, please. I've .... cleaned it.
8 She's .... been on three trips this year.

3 Use the cues to make dialogues with *already, just* and *yet*.

1 A: you/check/passport?
    Have you checked your passport yet?
   B: Yes, but (not/pack rucksack).
    Yes, but I haven't ...
2 A: your friend Sam/pick up/tickets?
   B: No, but .... (already/buy/them).
3 A: you/decide/take/phone or tablet?
   B: Yes, ... (just/pack it).
4 A: your friend Sam/book/taxi?
   B: No, but .... (yet/have got the number).
5 A: you/write down/emergency number?
   B: Yes, ... (just/write/the notepaper).

4 🔊 1.43 Complete the text using the words in brackets and the present perfect. Then listen and check.

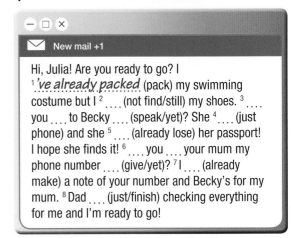

New mail +1

Hi, Julia! Are you ready to go? I
¹ *'ve already packed* (pack) my swimming costume but I ² .... (not find/still) my shoes. ³ .... you .... to Becky .... (speak/yet)? She ⁴ .... (just phone) and she ⁵ .... (already lose) her passport! I hope she finds it! ⁶ .... you .... your mum my phone number .... (give/yet)? ⁷ I .... (already make) a note of your number and Becky's for my mum. ⁸ Dad .... (just/finish) checking everything for me and I'm ready to go!

Your turn

5 Use the activities in the box to write five questions using *already, still, just* and *yet*.

> brush your teeth   do all your homework
> watch TV   play computer games
> tidy your room   read a book
> send a text message   take a photo

Have you brushed your teeth yet?

6 Ask and answer your questions with your partner. The person who gets the most *Yes* answers wins.

Have you brushed your teeth yet?

Yes, I have. / No, I haven't.

incredible! We've seen dolphins and turtles. We haven't seen any whales yet, but the captain says there are whales near the Spanish coast. This is definitely the best thing I've ever done!'

If you want to know more about the Tall Ships Youth Trust, visit their website at www.tallships.org

FACT! *Over 95,000 people have sailed 1.8 million nautical miles with the Tall Ships Youth Trust.*

Learn about Magellan the explorer.
- Why did Magellan go to live with the king and queen of Portugal?
- Why did Europeans want to go to Asia?
- What was Magellan's plan? Did he succeed?

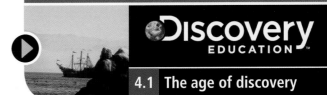

Discovery EDUCATION™

4.1 The age of discovery

Listening An interview

1 **Work with a partner. Look at the photo of some teenagers on a school trip in Paris. What kind of things do you think they've done on their trip so far?**

2 🔊 **1.44 Listen to the conversations. Which sentence best summarises how the teenagers feel about the trip?**

a They all love everything about the trip.

b They think the trip is really boring.

c They like some things on the trip more than others.

3 🔊 **1.44 Listen again and answer the questions.**

1 When did they arrive?

2 How long have they been in Paris?

3 How did they get to the top of the Eiffel Tower?

4 Have they visited any museums?

5 Have they done any shopping?

6 How's their French?

7 When is their last day?

8 What do they want to do on their last day?

Vocabulary Phrasal verbs

4 🔊 **1.45 Match the phrasal verbs (1–6) with their synonyms (a–f). Then listen, check and repeat.**

1 I really want to **come back**.

2 We've **picked up** lots of French.

3 Our bus **set off** at 5 am.

4 They want us to **find out** for ourselves.

5 We're going to **look round** the shops.

6 We've been so busy, we all just want to **chill out**.

a discover   d learn in an informal way

b explore   e start on a journey

c relax   f return

> 👁 **Get it right!**
>
> We can separate some phrasal verbs. Use a good dictionary to check.
> We've **picked up** a lot of French.
> We've **picked** a lot of French **up**.
> With object pronouns we say:
> We picked **it** up. (not ~~We picked up it~~.)

5 **Complete the sentences with the correct form of the verbs in Exercise 4.**

1 On the guided tour of the museum, we ...*found out*... all about tall ships.

2 While my dad was in Argentina, he .... a bit of Spanish.

3 While I .... that bookshop, I found this travel guide for Dublin.

4 This is a terrible restaurant. I don't think I will .... here ever again!

5 You're really nervous. Why don't you .... ?

6 We have to .... early if we want to get to Cambridge before lunch.

➡ **Say it right!** • page 96

Your turn

6 **Think of a place you visited. Make notes. Try to use the phrasal verbs.**

I've visited Rome in Italy. I didn't pick up any Italian.

7 **Ask and answer about the place you visited with your partner.**

➡ **Vocabulary Bank** • page 110

Language focus 2 Present perfect with *for* or *since*

1 Complete the examples from the listening on page 44. Then complete the rules.

	two days. five minutes. a long time. three years.
We've been here	
1	
2	Tuesday. three o'clock. March. 2012.

We use .... with periods of time and .... when we talk about a specific time.

➡ Grammar reference • page 102

2 Look at the table and complete the sentences with *for* or *since*.

1 I've been in Paris .... two days and I haven't seen the Eiffel Tower yet!

2 We set off early but we've only been on the bus .... an hour.

3 I haven't seen our teachers .... 10 o'clock this morning.

4 I'd love to go to Disneyland Paris – I haven't been there .... I was five.

5 I have studied French .... five years and I can understand quite a lot.

6 Helen's picked up a lot of French .... she's been in Paris.

7 We haven't eaten any French food .... we got here!

8 My teacher hasn't been to Paris .... ten years and she's a bit lost!

Present perfect and past simple

3 Complete the examples from the listening on page 44.

A: When ¹ *did* you .... (get) here?

B: On Tuesday, we ² .... (set off) at 5 am! We ³ .... (be) here for two full days. This is our third day

A: ⁴ .... you .... (be) up the tower yet?

B: Yes, we ⁵ .... (go) up about an hour ago.

➡ Grammar reference • page 102

4 🔊 1.48 Choose the correct words to complete the text. Then listen and check.

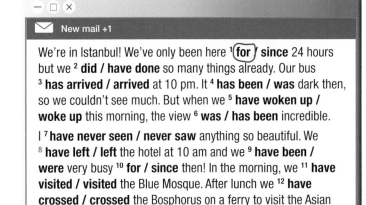

✉ New mail +1

We're in Istanbul! We've only been here ¹(**for**)/ **since** 24 hours but we ² **did / have done** so many things already. Our bus ³ **has arrived / arrived** at 10 pm. It ⁴ **has been / was** dark then, so we couldn't see much. But when we ⁵ **have woken up / woke up** this morning, the view ⁶ **was / has been** incredible.

I ⁷ **have never seen / never saw** anything so beautiful. We ⁸ **have left / left** the hotel at 10 am and we ⁹ **have been / were** very busy ¹⁰ **for / since** then! In the morning, we ¹¹ **have visited / visited** the Blue Mosque. After lunch we ¹² **have crossed / crossed** the Bosphorus on a ferry to visit the Asian side of the city. We ¹³ **haven't had / didn't have** anything to eat ¹⁴ **for / since** lunchtime. It's 9 pm and I'm really hungry! It's time for supper!

Bye for now,

Your turn

5 Ask and answer with a partner. Choose one of the phrases in box A. Continue the conversations using phrases in box B.

A

> set off on a journey very early   visit a really big city
> go on a school trip   go to a theme park

B

> When did you go?   What did you do?
> Who did you go with?   Where did you go?
> What did you eat?   Did you like it?

A: *Have you ever set off ... ?*
B: *Yes, I have.*
A: *Where did you go?*
B: *I went to ...*

Discover Culture

1 Look at the photos. Do you know what they are?

2 Work with a partner. What do you know about Australia? Make a list of other images you might see in the video.

Australia

Find out about Australia.

◉Discovery
EDUCATION™

4.2 The strange and beautiful land of Australia

3 ▶ 4.2 Watch the video. Which images did you see in Exercise 1? Make a list of the other things that you saw under the categories below.

1 famous places   2 animals   3 sports

4 ▶ 4.2 Watch the video again. Complete the sentences with the correct words.

1 Uluru is a giant .... near Sydney.
2 People first brought .... to Australia in the ....
3 In the national park you can see ...., ... and wombats.
4 .... shearing is popular all over the country.
5 Cane .... are poisonous.
6 Australian rules football is very similar to ....

5 Match these adjectives with the things that they describe in the video.

confusing   unusual   famous   poisonous

1 Uluru   3 toads
2 camel-racing   4 Australian rules football

6 ▶ 4.2 What other information did you hear about these things? Watch the video again and check your answers.
Millions of people travel to Australia every year.

7 What is the video about? Choose the best summary.

a unusual things in Australia
b well-known things about Australia
c well-known and unusual things in Australia

Your turn

8 Ask and answer the questions with your partner.

1 Would you like to go to Australia? Why/Why not?
2 What landmarks, animals and sports are special to your own country?

Reading A poster presentation

1 Work with a partner. Look at the photos of New Zealand. What do you think life is like there?

2 🔊 **1.49** Read the presentation. Whose culture and customs are important in New Zealand?

3 Read the presentation again. Match the headings with the correct paragraphs.

A Education   D New Zealand identity
B Art   E The perfect view
C Getting active

Explore interesting adjectives

4 Complete the sentences with the adjectives from the text.

1 an ...*important*... part of New Zealand's identity
2 has .... landscapes
3 their .... *haka*
4 Cricket is incredibly ....
5 One of the most .... art forms

5 Use the adjectives from Exercise 4 to describe your own country.

Football/Skiing is an important sport …

➡ **Vocabulary Bank** • page 110

Your turn

6 Make notes about another country.

1 What are the people and landscape like?
2 What do you know about their sports and art?
3 Do you know anything about their education system?

The people are very friendly and the landscape is beautiful. I know they like football a lot. Many famous artists come from here. I don't really know much about the education system.

7 Ask and answer the questions from Exercise 6 with your partner. Ask him/her if he/she can help you to collect more information.

> Do you know anything about the education system in Spain?

New Zealand

New Zealand

❶ ...*D New Zealand identity*...
The first people to arrive about 1,000 years ago were from Eastern Polynesia. Their culture and their customs developed into the Maori way of life – this has been an important part of New Zealand's identity ever since.

❷ ....
New Zealand has amazing landscapes with high mountains and over 3,800 lakes! There are at least twelve active volcanoes. The largest lake in New Zealand, Lake Taupo, lies in the crater of one of the biggest volcanoes on Earth. More than 30% of New Zealand is forest.

❸ ....
New Zealanders love sports. The most famous sport is rugby – the All Blacks are famous for their spectacular haka, the Maori challenge dance before their international matches. Cricket is also incredibly popular. With 6,000 kilometres of coastline it also means water sports are very popular – sailing, kayaking, diving and surfing.

❹ ....
One of the most striking art forms in Maori culture is the Ta moko, Maori tattoos. The design is incredibly complicated and they are made by tapping the needle into the skin. Maori men often have Ta moko on their faces and Maori women have them on their lips and chins.

❺ ....
New Zealanders have to go to school from the age of six until they are 16. The school year starts in January or February and finishes in the middle of December. There are four terms with two-week holidays between each term. The school day starts at nine o'clock and finishes at three o'clock.

FACT! *The human population of New Zealand is 4 million. The sheep population is 36 million.*

Speaking Signing up for an activity

Real talk: What's the most exciting thing you've ever done?

1 ▶ **4.3** Watch the teenagers in the video. What activities do they talk about?

- river rafting
- canyoning
- skiing
- walking behind a waterfall
- jumping into water
- sailing
- playing in a concert
- going on a rollercoaster

2 💬 What's the most exciting thing *you've* ever done?

3 🔊 **1.50** Listen to Gemma talking to an activity guide. What is she going to do?

4 Complete the conversation with the useful language.

Useful language

Where can I sign up?
Can I ask you a few things about (…)?
What about … ?
What do I need to bring?
How long is … ?
Does the price include (…)?

5 🔊 **1.50** Listen again and check your answers.

6 💬 Work with a partner. Practise the conversation in Exercise 4.

7 💬 Change the words in bold in the conversation. Use the ideas below. Take turns to ask and answer the questions.

REGIS RIVER RAFTING

Whitewater rafting with qualified instructors
We provide: wetsuit, life jacket and helmet, hot drinks
You bring: swimsuit and towel, warm clothes
From beginners to advanced
Morning (9–12) or afternoon (3–6)

REGIS

TREKKING TOURS

Trekking with qualified instructors
We provide: maps, picnic lunch, transport
You bring: boots, warm clothes, a camera
Everyone welcome
All day (10–5)

Gemma:	Can I ¹ ___*ask you*___ a few things about the canyoning trip?
Guide:	The **Blue Canyon** one? Sure. What would you like to know?
Gemma:	Well, is it only for people who've already done it?
Guide:	No, you don't need any experience. We give training with qualified guides, and the **Blue Canyon** is fine for **beginners**.
Gemma:	Great! ² … need to bring? I haven't got a wetsuit or anything.
Guide:	That's OK. We provide a **wetsuit, helmet, shoes and life jacket**. Just bring **your swimsuit** and **towel** and **some warm clothes for after**.
Gemma:	OK, good! How ³ … is the trip to **Blue Canyon**?
Guide:	It's **all day**, from **nine until six**.
Gemma:	I see. ⁴ … **food**, then? Does the price ⁵ … ?
Guide:	**Food is included** in the price. We look after everything, so you just enjoy the adventure!
Gemma:	Wow! It sounds fantastic. Where ⁶ … sign up?
Guide:	Right here!

✎ Writing A travel blog

1 **Look at the photos and read Mitch's blog. Where is he on holiday?**

Mitch's holiday blog: Highway 101 Road Trip

What an amazing holiday! We've been on the road in our camper van for ten days, and since we left LA we've driven over 700 km, so we've already done half the trip. I had an extra waffle for breakfast to celebrate! Definitely my favourite place up to now has been Hearst Castle – what incredible buildings!

Today was another fantastic drive up the coast from Santa Cruz (where we stayed the night) to San Francisco. I've seen lots of pictures of the Golden Gate Bridge so I was very excited but … we didn't cross it!! Mum says it's on the *other* side of San Francisco so I haven't seen it yet. What a big disappointment!

Bye till tomorrow.

2 **Read the blog again and answer the questions.**
1 How many days has he been travelling?
2 How far has he travelled?
3 What places has he visited?
4 What has been his favourite place?
5 What has/hasn't he seen?

Useful language

Expressing how you feel, good or bad.
Use interesting activities to write about how you feel.
* *What an amazing holiday!* (or *What a holiday!*)
* *What incredible buildings!*

3 **Look at the Useful language box. Find one example of how Mitch feels bad in the blog.**

4 **Complete the exclamations using the nouns (1–6) and a good (☺) or bad (☹) adjective from the box.**

> beautiful   boring   comfortable   delicious   exciting   ugly

1 waffles ☺
   What delicious waffles!
2 trip ☹
   What a boring trip!
3 film ☺
4 beds ☺
5 building ☹
6 photos ☺

✎ Get writing

PLAN

5 **Make notes about a holiday blog post. Include information from Exercise 2 to help you.**

WRITE

6 **Write your holiday blog post. Use your notes and the model text to help you.**

CHECK

7 **Can you say YES to these questions?**
* Is the information from Exercise 2 in your blog post?
* Have you included one or two exclamations to say how you feel?

49

3–4 Review

Vocabulary

1 Complete the sentences with the words in the box.

> buskers ~~graffiti~~ exhibition
> sculptures living statue concert hall

1 There's some amazing _graffiti_ on the wall outside the library.
2 We often go to our local .... to hear classical music or opera.
3 I love .... that are made of stone or metal.
4 Did you see those ....? They're playing music in the park.
5 I went to an .... of modern art yesterday.
6 Have you seen the .... in the main square? You give him some money and he moves!

2 Write the names of the musical instruments.

saxophone

3 Complete the sentences with the phrases in the box and the correct form of *go*, *go on* or *go to*.

> ~~climbing~~ sailing a safari a guided tour
> a summer camp trekking

1 We _go climbing_ every summer in the mountains.
2 They .... when they were in Italy. They walked 20 km a day.
3 I love .... – you can make new friends and learn new skills.
4 Jim is .... of Cambridge tomorrow. An expert takes you round and tells you the history of the city.
5 Do you want to .... at the weekend? It's very relaxing on the boat.
6 I'd love to .... and see wild animals, but it's very expensive.

4 Choose the correct word.

1 When did they come (back)/ up from their trip?
2 I picked **out / up** a bit of Italian on holiday.
3 They want to set **up / off** early in the morning.
4 I usually chill **up / out** in front of the TV at the weekend.
5 Where can we find **out / off** about day trips?
6 Let's look **out / around** the town while we're waiting.

Explore vocabulary

5 Complete the sentences with the words in the box. Use the correct form when necessary.

> dress up post online show up take it in turns
> first taste keep watch ~~make money~~ disabled

1 I drew portraits at the school fair and I _made_ a lot of _money_.
2 When I was on the summer camp, I had my .... of climbing.
3 Kate .... late to the party. She missed the bus.
4 Can you .... those photos .... so I can see them?
5 What costume are you .... in to go to the party?
6 My little brothers always argue over toys, they can't .... to play with something.
7 When we went on a safari the guide .... at night for wild animals.
8 The theme park is great for .... people too – there aren't any steps and there's extra help if you need it.

6 Complete the text with the words in the box.

> ~~perfect~~ pick up passionate about
> take photos amazing cool stuff
> popular important

Ireland is the [1]_perfect_ place to take a holiday. There is lots of [2].... to do for everyone like trekking in the [3].... countryside or visiting the beautiful cities of Dublin or Cork. Music is an [4].... part of Irish identity and the Irish are [5].... music and dance. You can see traditional music played in places all over Dublin. There are lots of opportunities to [6]...., for example the Giant's Causeway – it is incredibly [7].... with photographers and tourists. Many people in Ireland speak Irish, but if you think you will [8].... a little Irish, think again – it's very hard!

Language focus

1 Complete the email with the verbs in the box. Use the present perfect.

see	go	record	~~visit~~	not go	buy	take

> **New mail +1**
>
> Hi Janice,
> We're having a lovely time here in Paris. We
> ¹*have visited* five art galleries and two museums.
> I ² .... never .... such wonderful art! We ³ .... to
> several lectures about modern art. I ⁴ .... them for
> you so you can listen later! Tony ⁵ .... hundreds of
> photos and he ⁶ .... a lot of posters and postcards!
> We ⁷ .... to the Picasso Museum – that's tomorrow.
> See you soon,
> Angie

2 Complete the conversation with the present perfect and *ever* or *never*. Use the verbs in brackets.

Mike:	This music is from South Africa. ¹*have* you *ever heard* (hear) this kind of music?
Kevin:	Yes, I have. There's a concert tomorrow. ² .... you .... (go) to a concert of African music?
Mike:	No, I ³ .... (go) to a live concert.
Kevin:	Can you play any musical instruments?
Mike:	I can play the piano and my brother plays the guitar.
Kevin:	⁴ .... he .... (play) in any concerts?
Mike:	Yes, but I ⁵ .... (see) him play.

3 Complete the sentences with *for* or *since*.

1 I haven't seen Jim *for* a long time.
2 I've lived here .... a year.
3 I've picked up a lot of Spanish .... January.
4 We haven't had any homework .... Monday.
5 She's been in bed .... ten days – she's very ill.
6 She hasn't visited her friend .... weeks.

4 Complete the conversations with the verbs in brackets. Use the present perfect or past simple.

1 A: ¹*Have you been* (be) to New York?
   B: Yes, we ² .... (go) there last year.
2 A: How long ³ .... Sarah .... (live) in Rome?
   B: She ⁴ .... (move) there six months ago.
3 A: What time ⁵ .... you .... (arrive)?
   B: We ⁶ .... (not be) here for very long – about ten minutes.

Language builder

5 Choose the correct words to complete the text.

> Hi Keira!
>
> How are you? I ¹ *a* this email to you in the hotel
> café in Prague – we've ² .... got back from the
> main square. We ³ .... here ⁴ .... two days and we
> have ⁵ .... quite a lot. My Dad ⁶ .... lots of photos
> and he takes ages so we always ⁷ .... wait for him.
> Yesterday while we ⁸ .... for my Dad, we ⁹ ....
> some ice cream in a really cool art café. Prague is
> a beautiful city – you ¹⁰ ....
> come here some time! OK,
> Mum and Sam are back – we
> haven't had dinner ¹¹ .... .
> Talk later!
>
> Fiona

1	a	am writing	b	write	c have written
2	a	yet	b	just	c already
3	a	have been	b	are	c have gone
4	a	since	b	for	c just
5	a	already seen	b	yet seen	c seen already
6	a	took	b	takes usually	c usually takes
7	a	should	b	must	c have to
8	a	have waited	b	were waiting	c waited
9	a	had	b	have had	c were having
10	a	should	b	have	c mustn't
11	a	just	b	already	c yet

Speaking

6 Match the sentences.

1 Shall I ask my mum to get us?   *b*
2 How long is the trip?
3 What do I need to bring?
4 What time shall we meet?
5 Where can I sign up?
6 Do you fancy going to a concert?

a It starts at 8 pm, so how about 7.30?
b Yes, that's a good idea.
c Yeah, why not?
d A towel and a swimming costume.
e It's all morning.
f Right here!

5 Let's talk

Social networks p55

The language of the future? p58

Giving a presentation p60

CLIL Pictures with meaning p119

Discovery EDUCATION™

In this unit ...

Vocabulary
- Communication
- Communication collocations
- Communication verbs
- Phrasal verbs

Language focus
- *will*, *might/may* + adverbs of possibility and probability: *definitely*, *probably*
- First conditional

Unit aims
I can ...
- describe different ways of communicating.
- talk about events that I'm sure and not sure about in the future.
- talk about possible situations in the future.
- understand about English as a world language.
- reassure someone.
- write an essay about the best way to communicate.

BE CURIOUS

What can you see in the photo?
Start thinking
- What are the children doing?
- Are they communicating with each other?
- What do you think about how they are communicating?

Vocabulary
Communication

1 🔊 **2.01** Match the words in the box with the pictures (a–f). Which pictures are missing? Then listen, check and repeat.

> Tweet   text message   social media post
> email   ~~chatting~~   phone call   Skype™
> forum   blog post

a   *chatting*

2 Match the missing pictures from Exercise 1 to the definitions.

1   A message of 140 characters.
2   When you write information about yourself to share with others.
3   An online diary.

3 Match the comments with a form of communication from the box in Exercise 1.

1   Hi, this is Susan. Sorry, I can't talk at the moment. Please leave me a message after the beep! *phone call*
2   Please find attached the form. You need to complete it and send it back to me.
3   Hi Grandma, can you see me OK? I can hear you but there's no video. Can you turn your webcam on?
4   @RM_Players celebrate in the street. We won the league again! #victory
5   OK Tanya, CU on Fri at 7:30 @ the cinema. Txt me if u get lost!
6   Barbara has added 17 new photos to her album Life in Leeds.

4 🔊 **2.02** Listen to the conversation. What forms of communication do they talk about from Exercise 1?

Your turn

5 Put the forms of communication from Exercise 1 in order of when you most often use them.

6 Work with a partner. Compare your answers from Exercise 5. Then complete the quiz and compare your answers.

> I've got text messages first because I send hundreds of texts every day!

1 How often do you use these forms of communication?

	several times a day	once a day	once a week	less
phone				
email				
text				
Tweet				
Skype™				

2 What do you usually post on social media, Twitter or blogs?

☐ my life   ☐ school   ☐ news
☐ jokes   ☐ photos
☐ other (please specify) ....

➡ **Vocabulary Bank • page 111**

Reading A survey

1 Work with a partner. Look at the photo. Is the situation familiar to you?

2 🔊 **2.03** Read the introduction to an online survey. What is it about?

a face-to-face communication
b teenagers and communication
c teenagers and computers

3 🔊 **2.04** Read the survey. Then work with a partner, answer the questions and read the results.

HOW DO YOU COMMUNICATE?

A recent survey showed that although 80% of UK teens have more than 400 Facebook friends, they have only met a quarter of these friends in real life. Psychologists worry that teens in the future might lose the ability to make friends face-to-face and will only communicate through Tweets, online forums and status updates. Is that true for you? Complete our social networking survey and find out!

1 WHAT'S THE BEST WAY TO MAKE FRIENDS?
A Social networking sites like Facebook and Twitter.
B It depends on the person.
C Face-to-face.

2 HOW WILL SOCIAL NETWORKS CHANGE IN THE NEXT TEN YEARS?
A They will get more popular.
B There will probably be a lot more of them.
C They definitely won't disappear but people might get bored with them and go back to chatting over a coffee.

3 IS THERE A DANGER OF HAVING TOO MANY ONLINE FRIENDS?
A No, it's how the digital generation meet.
B It depends on how many real-life friends you have.
C Yes, people might forget how to communicate in real life.

4 WHICH SENTENCE MIGHT BE TRUE FOR YOU IN FIVE YEARS' TIME?
A You'll certainly have a lot more online friends.
B You'll have the same number of friends both online and in real life.
C You may need to start making friends online.

Explore communication collocations

4 Match the words and phrases from the survey with the definitions below.

> status update   face-to-face   virtual friends
> digital generation   social network sites

1 a post about your current activity, thoughts or feelings
2 group of people who have grown up with digital technology
3 people you can see and speak to on a computer
4 directly, meeting in the same place
5 a website that helps people communicate and share information

➡ **Vocabulary Bank • page 111**

Your turn

5 Discuss the following statements. Do you agree or disagree?

Most of my friends …

a communicate through their status updates every day.
b access social networks by phone or tablet.
c have met their virtual friends (on social media, Twitter etc.) in real life.
d don't have a social network account but they would like to have one.

RESULTS

Mostly A: You love social media (but you may love it too much). You're great at making virtual friends. But what about real life? Do you have enough friends there too?

Mostly B: You like to use a bit of both. You have a good mixture of online and real-life friends.

Mostly C: You prefer face-to-face communication but you also know you might need to use social networks for your job or studies one day.

FACT! *Facebook has over 1 billion active users. 30% of them are in Europe.*

Language focus 1 *will, might/may* + adverbs of possibility

1 Look at the examples from the text on page 54. Write (C) certain or (NC) not certain. Then complete the rules.

a They **will get** more popular. *C*

b You **may need** to start making friends online.

c There **will probably be** a lot more of them.

d They **definitely won't** disappear.

e You'll **certainly have** a lot more online friends.

f They **might not** disappear.

> We use ¹.... and ².... to show we are sure about the future. We use ³.... / .... to show we are not sure about the future. We use *probably*, *definitely* and *certainly* to show how sure we are.

➡ Grammar reference • page 103

2 Complete the sentences. Use the verbs and prompts in brackets to help you.

1 I'm sure everyone .....*will have*..... an Internet connection in the future. (*have* – certain)

2 I .... my mobile phone next month, I'm not sure yet. (*change* – not certain)

3 My brother .... ever .... all his friends on social media, it's impossible, he's got too many! (*meet* – certain)

4 I don't know, I .... tonight – I have a lot of work to do. (*go online* – not certain)

5 My grandparents .... definitely .... me later, it's cheaper than a phone call. (*Skype*™ – certain)

6 Our teacher .... us next week, so you should listen. (*test* – not certain)

3 Use the prompts to write sentences using your own ideas. Use the adverbs *definitely*, *probably* and *certainly* in the correct position.

1 social networks / with us / for a long time. *Social networks will definitely be with us for a long time.*

2 lose contact / friends you have now

3 make / new friends in the future

4 tablets / more popular than smartphones in the future

5 online friends / not replace real-life friends in my lifetime

4 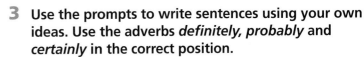 **2.05** Complete the blog post with the words in the box. Then listen, check and repeat.

> will (x3)   won't   probably   might (x3)

A techno geek speaks out:

In the near future, machines ¹.....*will*..... do everything for us. There ².... be any books, only screens. We ³.... won't need teachers, because we ⁴.... definitely be able to learn everything on our own. I imagine that some of you ⁵.... not like the idea because you're frightened of change, but it's good! As for communication, who knows, we ⁶.... see the end of telephones. I'm not sure but I think television ⁷.... disappear too – we ⁸.... probably watch everything on our computers!

Your turn

5 Make predictions about your lives. Use *will, might/may* and adverbs of probability. Write five sentences.

My family will probably visit a foreign country in the future.
Our teacher will definitely give us homework tonight.

6 Work with a partner. Compare and discuss your ideas.

> Learn about communicating online.
> What social network sites do you use?
> Which three social networks do they talk about in the video?
> Why are they 'changing the Internet'?

DISCOVERY EDUCATION™

5.1 Social networks

Vocabulary
Communication verbs

1 🔊 **2.06** **Complete the sentences with the correct form of the words in the box. Then listen and check.**

> whisper   complain   boast   gossip   ~~argue~~
> joke   shout   criticise

1 Don't ..... *argue* ..... with me – you know that I'm right!
2 You shouldn't .... about the bad weather – what do you expect in England in November!
3 I don't like him. He's always .... about people behind their backs.
4 It's true that she does well at school, but she doesn't need to .... about it.
5 You shouldn't .... with your friends about something serious. They might not think it's funny.
6 Emmet is my friend, so don't .... him. And anyway, nobody's perfect!
7 Sshh! I'm trying to study. If you want to talk, please .... !
8 Those boys are always ..... . They're so noisy!!

Your turn

2 **Make notes about three of the situations.**

1 a time when you argued with someone
2 the last time you complained about something
3 the last time someone criticised you
4 a time when someone shouted at you
5 someone you know who boasts a lot
6 a time when you joked with someone and they didn't think it was funny

I argued with my brother last week. It was about the computer.

My teacher criticised me yesterday because I forgot my homework again.

3 **Ask and answer with your partner about your situations. Find out more information.**

A: When was the last time you argued with someone?
B: I argued with my sister about the computer.
A: Why did you argue about the computer?

➡ **Vocabulary Bank • page 111**

Listening   Short conversations

4 **Work with a partner. Look at the photos of four different conversations and answer the questions.**

1 Where are the people?
2 What is the relationship between them?
3 What do you think they are talking about?

5 🔊 **2.07** **Listen to four short conversations. Match the photos in Exercise 4 to the conversations.**

6 🔊 **2.07** **Listen again. Answer the questions.**

Conversation 1
1 What is Serena's problem?
2 What does her mother promise?

Conversation 2
1 What does Alex want Nick to do?
2 What's Alex's opinion of football?

Conversation 3
1 What does Bella say about Rachel?
2 What is Tina's reaction?

Conversation 4
1 When does the concert start?
2 How does Paul make his friend hurry up?

Language focus 2 First Conditional + *may/might, be able to*

1 **Complete the examples from the listening on page 56.**

1 If you .*pass*. all your exams,
we.*'ll have*. a holiday abroad this year.

2 We .... in the cup final **if we win** tonight.

3 If you **wear** make-up, they .... **send** you home.

4 If you .... first in the queue, you**'ll get** to meet the band!

5 You .... the band if you**'re** late.

2 **Look at the examples again. Use the words in the box to change or add more information.**

definitely send   may have   be able to
probably meet   might miss

1 If you pass all your exams, we .... a holiday abroad this year.

2 We'll .... be in the cup final if we win tonight.

3 If you wear make-up to school, they'll .... you home.

4 If you're first in the queue you'll .... the band.

5 You .... the band if you're late.

3 **Look at the examples in Exercises 1 and 2 and choose the words to complete the rules.**

1 We use the first conditional to talk about possible situations in the *past / future*.

2 We can use *might/may*, and *be able to* instead of *will / the present simple*.

3 When we use adverbs they come *before / after* the verb.

 Grammar reference • page 103

Get it right!

When the *if* clause comes first, it ends with a comma (,).
If we meet the band, I'll be really happy.

4 **Use the prompts to write sentences.**

1 you whisper / not be able to hear you
If you whisper, she won't be able to hear you.

2 if / you post an update / I definitely / read it

3 I / text you / if / get lost

4 if / she speak quickly / I might not / understand

5 you / might make / new friends / if / join the club

6 if / they practise a lot / be able to win

5 **Complete the text with the correct form of the verbs in brackets.**

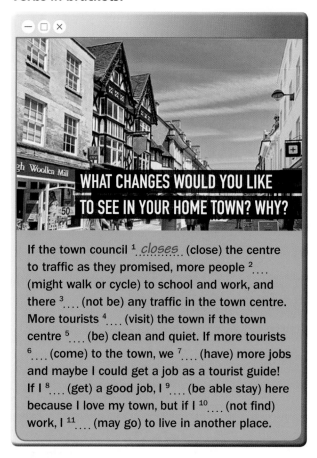

WHAT CHANGES WOULD YOU LIKE TO SEE IN YOUR HOME TOWN? WHY?

If the town council [1] *closes* (close) the centre to traffic as they promised, more people [2] .... (might walk or cycle) to school and work, and there [3] .... (not be) any traffic in the town centre. More tourists [4] .... (visit) the town if the town centre [5] .... (be) clean and quiet. If more tourists [6] .... (come) to the town, we [7] .... (have) more jobs and maybe I could get a job as a tourist guide! If I [8] .... (get) a good job, I [9] .... (be able stay) here because I love my town, but if I [10] .... (not find) work, I [11] .... (may go) to live in another place.

➡ **Say it right! • page 96**

Your turn

6 **Complete three of the sentences below so that they are true for you. Then write two more sentences.**

If the weather is good over the weekend, …
If I don't pass all my exams, …
If I have enough money, …
If I argue with my parents.
If I criticise my friend.
If I shout at my teacher.

If the weather is good over the weekend, I'll go out with my friends for a picnic. If we go out for a picnic, we'll probably take a guitar with us. If we take a guitar, I'll definitely sing some songs.

7 **Work with a partner. Compare your sentences.**

Discover Culture

1 Look at the photos. They refer to the two topics in the video about China. Think about the questions below.

1 What does China produce? Do you have any items produced in China with you now?

2 What languages do Chinese people speak?

China

MADE IN CHINA

Find out about Mandarin.

Discovery EDUCATION™

5.2 The language of the future

2 ▶ 5.2 Watch the video and check your answers.

3 ▶ 5.2 Watch the video again. What do you hear about these numbers?

1 1.4 billion   3 1950s
2 40,000   4 10 or 20 years

4 Watch the video again. Choose the correct answer.

1 China's population is bigger than
   a Europe's.   b the United States'.
   c Europe and the United States' together.

2 The Chinese people speak
   a different languages.   b Mandarin.   c English.

3 In written Mandarin, people use
   a 40,000 characters.   b three or four thousand characters.
   c four thousand characters.

4 The Pinyin system uses
   a the Roman alphabet.   b Chinese characters.   c a computer.

5 More people speak .... in the world than English.
   a Mandarin   b Roman   c French

5 Test your memory. What did you see when you heard these phrases?

1 Everything in China is growing.

2 The country produces so many things.

3 Every day, more and more people use Mandarin to communicate.

6 ▶ 5.2 Watch the video again and check your answers.

Your turn

7 Discuss the questions in groups.

1 What does your country produce? Does it go to many other countries?

2 Would you like to learn Mandarin? Why/Why not? Why would it be useful?

3 Is your language a difficult language to learn for foreign learners? Why?/Why not?

Reading An article

1 **Work with a partner. Look at the pictures and answer the questions.**

1 Where would you see the images?

2 Why do you think they are in English?

2 🔊 **2.10** **Read the article about the English language. Is English still the world's number one language?**

3 **Read the article again. Mark the sentences true (T) or false (F). Correct the false ones.**

1 English is everywhere because a lot of people understand it.

2 There are fewer second language speakers of English than native speakers.

3 In Denmark, people speak English as a second language.

4 The English language has the most words.

5 *Selfie* and *app* are old words.

6 The author is sure that Mandarin will be the world's next number one language.

Explore phrasal verbs

4 **Look at the highlighted words in the text. Match the phrasal verbs in the box to the definitions.**

> go up   get by   keep on   come into use   turn into

1 When a figure or number increases or gets bigger.

2 Start being used.

3 When something changes and becomes something different.

4 To be able to live with a situation with difficulty.

5 When you continue to do something.

➡ **Vocabulary Bank • page 111**

Your turn

5 **Complete the sentences about English with your own ideas. Then compare your sentences.**

1 I enjoy/don't enjoy learning English because …

2 Learning English is difficult because …

3 I sometimes use English …

4 I think in the future I will use English …

I enjoy learning because I like talking to …

THE WORLD OF ENGLISH

Almost everywhere you go in the world, you'll see English. It's on signs, adverts and T-shirts! In the online world, it's even more obvious. Why? Because it is the one language that most people understand – more than Mandarin or Spanish, which have more native speakers than English.

So, how many people speak English? Right now there are over 360 million native speakers of English in the world. And a similar number of people speak it as a second language. But there are more than a billion people who speak or are learning English and that figure is **going up**. In countries like Denmark, Singapore or Israel more than 80% of people speak English. So, if you go there, you'll find it easy to **get by**!

There are also more words in English than in almost any other language. At the moment, there are over a million words in English and we **keep on** adding more words. You might know words like *selfie*, *Tweet*, *app* and *chillax*. All of these words have **come into use** in the English language in the last few years.

And what about the future? Will English always be the world's number one language? For the moment, yes, but if the Chinese economy continues to grow, will Mandarin **turn into** the next number one world language? We'll have to wait and see!

FACT! *Soon there will be more people in China who speak English as a foreign language than there are native English speakers in the whole world!*

Speaking Reassuring someone

Real talk: Have you ever given a class presentation?

1 ▶ **5.3** Watch the teenagers in the video. How many teenagers …

a) have given a class presentation?
b) are nervous or worried about giving class presentations?
c) have to do class presentations regularly?

2 💬 Have *you* ever given a class presentation?

3 🔊 **2.11** Helen is talking to her older sister Petra. What is Helen worried about?

4 Complete the conversation with the useful language.

Useful language

Don't worry!	It'll turn out all right.
You don't need to worry.	There's no problem!
You'll be fine (I'm sure).	Of course you can (do it)!
Listen, I think I can help you.	

Petra: What's the matter Helen? You look worried.

Helen: I've got to **give a presentation in English class next week**, and I'm scared. I don't think I can do it!

Petra: Of ¹ ....*course*.... you can! **You're good at English**. You ² .... to worry.

Helen: Yes, but you know I'm really **shy**. It's **frightening in front of all those people!**

Petra: True, it's not easy if you're **shy**, but don't ³ ....! You'll ⁴ ...., I'm sure.

Helen: Well, the problem is, when I **speak in class** I feel **embarrassed and go red**. Then I **mix up the words**.

Petra: Hmm! Listen, I think I can ⁵ .... . Have you **written the presentation** yet?

Helen: Well, yes, I've **more or less finished it.**

Petra: Then ⁶ .... no problem! You can practise it **on me and my friends.**

Helen: OK! That sounds like a good idea. I'll feel more confident then.

Petra: Yes. If you practise it lots of times, I know it'll turn out ⁷ .... .

5 🔊 **2.11** Listen again and check your answers.

6 💬 Work with a partner. Practise the conversation in Exercise 4.

7 💬 Change the words in bold in the conversation. Use the ideas below. Take turns to ask and answer the questions.

Problem 1

You have to sing a song at the talent competition.

Problem 2

You are playing in the final of a tennis competition.

✎ Writing An essay

1 Look at the photo and read the essay. Choose the best title.

a Have mobile phones improved communication for teenagers?

b Are teenagers too dependent on mobile phones?

Twenty years ago, mobile phones were for business people. Nowadays, it's impossible to find a teenager without one, but are mobiles the best way for teenagers to communicate? Mobiles can be useful. Firstly, they allow teenagers to communicate with their friends and family anywhere, anytime. Sending text messages is also quick and cheap. What's more, mobiles help you organise your life, and you can tell your parents what you're doing so they don't worry.

However, there are negatives. For one thing, you might not have a signal, especially in the countryside. In addition, if you are in a noisy place, you can't hear your mobile ring. Lastly, using it all the time can be expensive.

On balance, I think mobiles have definitely improved communication for teenagers. Nevertheless, they mustn't use them too much.

2 Read the essay again. Answer the questions.

1 How does the writer get the reader's attention in the introduction?

2 How many arguments in favour of mobile phones are there?

3 How many arguments against mobile phones are there?

4 What is his/her opinion of mobile phones for teenagers?

Useful language

Introducing points and arguments

Use adverbs and other phrases to introduce what you want to say.

Nowadays, …	*What's more, …*	*Nevertheless,*
Firstly, …	*However, …*	

3 Look at the Useful language box. Find four other words or phrases to introduce arguments in the essay.

4 Complete the sentences with the words in the box.

> addition lastly more ~~one thing~~ Firstly

1 I recommend this mobile. For ....*one thing*...., it's a smartphone. What's ...., it's on special offer, and ...., it's quite small and light.

2 The new model has two improvements. ...., it has a much bigger memory, and in ...., the battery will last longer.

✎ Get writing

PLAN

5 Plan an essay. Include information from Exercise 4 to help you and the plan below.

Title: Are social networking sites like Facebook the best way for teenagers to communicate?

- an introduction
- a paragraph with arguments in favour
- a paragraph with arguments against
- a conclusion, including your opinion

WRITE

6 Write your essay. Use your notes from Exercise 5 and the model text to help you.

CHECK

7 Can you say YES to these questions?

- Is the information from the plan in your essay?
- Have you used expressions like *Firstly, What's more,* etc. in your essay?

6 Fears

Discovery EDUCATION

In this unit ...

Vocabulary
- Fears
- Prepositional phrases
  ending in *-ed* and *-ing*
- Opposites

Language focus
- *going to/will*/Present
  continuous
- Quantifiers

Unit aims
I can ...
- talk about fears.
- talk about things I will and won't do in
  the future.
- talk about how I feel.
- understand about superstitions.
- express surprise and disbelief.
- write an email to a friend about plans
  and problems.

BE CURIOUS

Look at the photo on this page.
What can you see in the photo?
Start thinking
- Where are the people?
- Why are they there?
- What isn't the man
  afraid of?

Vocabulary Fears

1 🔊 2.12 Match the words in the box with the photos of fears (a–g).
Which word is not in the photos? Then listen, check and repeat.

> flying   heights   ~~the dark~~   lifts   insects   birds   clowns   snakes

a *the dark*

2 🔊 2.13 Listen and match the speakers to the fears in Exercise 1.

1 *birds*

Your turn

3 How afraid are you of the things in Exercise 1? Put them in order.
Add one or two of your own fears to the list.

1 *heights*   2 *snakes*

4 Ask and answer with your partner. Compare your list.

1 Do you know anyone who has any of these fears or other common ones?
2 How does the fear change his/her behaviour?

My mum has a fear of flying. She drives really long distances to avoid going on a plane!

➡ **Vocabulary Bank** • page 112

63

Reading An advice column

1 Look at the photos. What do you think the teenagers are afraid of?

2 🔊 **2.14** Read the online advice column and check your answer.

3 Read the advice column again. Answer the questions.

1 What is the difference between a fear and a phobia?
2 Why does Isabella have to travel?
3 What is Mary's advice to Isabella?
4 Why does Kevin have to travel?
5 What is Kevin worried about?
6 What is Mary's advice to Kevin?

🔍 Explore prepositional phrases

4 Look at the highlighted phrases in the text. Complete the sentences with the correct prepositions after the verbs or adjectives.

1 My mother's terrified .... flying.
2 I'm very worried .... going up in the lift.
3 What do you think .... my new dress? Do you like it?
4 Are you going to share that chocolate .... me?
5 I'm a bit embarrassed .... my fear of insects.

➡️ **Vocabulary Bank • page 112**

👁 Get it right!

Advice doesn't have a plural form and cannot be used with *a* or *an*.
Maria gave good **advice**. ✓
Maria gave good **advices**. ✗
Maria gave a good advice. ✗

Your turn

5 Ask and answer with your partner.

1 Do you know of any other famous people who have fears or phobias? What are their fears?
2 Do you think Mary gave good advice? Do you think it's easy to help people with phobias? Why?/Why not?

Yes, I think … is afraid of …

Yes, I think it's very/quite good because she …

No, I don't think it's very good because …

I think it's easy/difficult to help people with phobias because …

ASK MARY

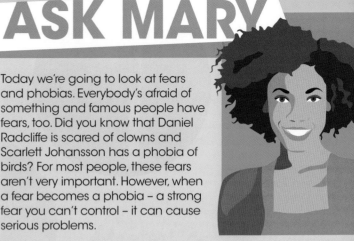

Today we're going to look at fears and phobias. Everybody's afraid of something and famous people have fears, too. Did you know that Daniel Radcliffe is scared of clowns and Scarlett Johansson has a phobia of birds? For most people, these fears aren't very important. However, when a fear becomes a phobia – a strong fear you can't control – it can cause serious problems.

ISABELLA, 13 (FLORIDA)

'My uncle's getting married next month and my parents and I are going to the wedding – in San Francisco! I'm **terrified of** flying and the flight takes four and a half hours. What am I going to do?'

Lots of people are afraid of flying. Jennifer Aniston, for example, hates planes, so you're in good company! Try to get some exercise before the flight so you'll feel tired and then you'll probably sleep on the plane. Listen to your favourite music. When you feel nervous, close your eyes and take long, deep breaths and you'll be fine!

KEVIN, 14 (LIVERPOOL)

'I can't sleep at night without a light. Next week, I'm travelling to London on a school trip and I'm going to **share a room with** other students. They'll definitely want to switch off the lights and I won't be able to sleep. I don't want them to think I'm a baby! Please help. I'm really **worried about** it!'

Don't be **embarrassed about** it. Did you know that Keanu Reeves is afraid of the dark? And no one says he's a baby! Don't worry about what other people will **think of** you. Just tell your roommates that you want a light on at night like it's the most normal thing in the world. They probably won't say anything about it.

FACT! *Arachnophobia, the fear of spiders, is the most common phobia. Millions of people around the world suffer from it.*

Language focus 1 *be going to/will*/Present continuous

1 **Match the sentences from the text on page 64 with the uses (a–c).**

1 I'm going to share a room with other students.
2 They probably **won't** say anything about it.
3 My uncle**'s getting** married next month.

a a definite arrangement
b a personal intention
c a prediction

➡ **Grammar reference • page 104**

2 **Join the parts of the sentences.**

1 We aren't going to
2 Don't watch that film
3 Are you going
4 Alice is flying to Spain
5 John's afraid of the dark so
6 I'm seeing our teacher

a to visit her aunty this summer.
b he'll probably sleep with the light on.
c take the lift.
d to watch a horror film this evening?
e at 4 pm about the school trip.
f or you'll have nightmares.

3 🔊 **2.15** **Choose the correct option to complete the conversation. Then listen and check.**

Sally: ¹ Will you fly /(Are you flying) to San Francisco next week?
Isa: Yes, the taxi ² **will arrive** / **is arriving** at 7 am!
Sally: And when's the wedding?
Isa: It's on Thursday. We ³ **are relaxing** / **'ll probably relax** on Wednesday – ⁴ I'm **going to go** / **I will go** shopping with my cousin in the day. Then in the evening, my aunty has booked a restaurant and we ⁵ **will eat** / **are eating** together at 8 pm.
Sally: And after the wedding? ⁶ **Will you** / **Are you going to** stay in San Francisco for a holiday?
Isa: No, we ⁷ **won't stay** / **aren't staying** very long – our flight back ⁸ **is leaving** / **will leave** on Saturday morning.

Your turn

4 **Make notes about the questions below.**

1 What job will you do when you're older?
2 When do you think you'll get married?
3 Will you still live in your town/village?
4 What are you doing after school today?
5 What are you going to do this weekend?
6 What are you going to do in the school holidays?

5 **Ask and answer with your partner. Use your notes from Exercise 4 to help you.**

> I think I'll be a doctor when I'm older.

> I think I'll be a teacher, but I'm not sure yet.

> This weekend, I'm going to watch a film with my friends.

Learn about a scary animal.
What do you think is the scariest animal?
What animal is the man trying to catch?
How does the man catch it?

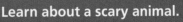

●Discovery
EDUCATION

6.1 **Creepy creatures**

Listening Conversations between friends

1 **Work with a partner. Look at the photo of the roller coaster and answer the questions.**

1 How do you think the people on the roller coaster are feeling?

2 The ride is called *The Scream Machine*. Why do you think so?

3 Do you like roller coasters? Why/Why not?

2 🔊 **2.16 Listen to two conversations between a group of friends in a theme park. How do Anita and Bruno feel a) at the beginning of the day and b) at the end of the day?**

3 🔊 **2.16 Listen again. Choose the correct answers.**

Conversation 1

1 Which ride is Anita scared of?

   a The Scream Machine   b The Colossus

   c The Tidal Wave

2 How does Bruno feel about The Tidal Wave?

   a He's terrified.   b He's worried.

   c He's relaxed.

3 Why does Claudia suggest starting with The Scream Machine?

   a The queue is short.   b It's very scary.

   c It's lots of fun.

Conversation 2

4 What was Claudia's favourite ride?

   a The Colossus   b The Tidal Wave

   c The Scream Machine

5 What is the problem at the end of the day?

   a They miss the bus home.

   b They've spent a lot of money.

   c They can't get anything to eat.

Vocabulary *-ed* and *-ing* adjectives

4 🔊 **2.17 Look at the pictures and example sentences. Circle the correct words. Then listen, check and repeat.**

I'm terrified.

It's terrifying.

1 I'm really (bored)/ boring. There's nothing to do!

2 The film we saw last night was **terrified / terrifying**!

3 Yesterday we looked at the physics of roller coasters in class. It was very **interested / interesting**.

4 We took my little cousins to a theme park at the weekend. They were really **excited / exciting**!

5 Yesterday we went on a 20-kilometre walk in the country. It was really **tired / tiring**!

6 I'm a bit **worried / worrying**. I have to give a presentation to the whole class tomorrow!

> 👁 **Get it right!**
>
> *I'm bored.* = how we feel
> *It's boring.* = something that causes that feeling
> We use *in* with *interested* and *of* with *afraid/scared/frightened/terrified*.
> *I'm very interested in snakes.*
> *Anita's terrified of roller coasters.*

Your turn

5 **Complete the sentences so that they're true for you.**

1 I'm really interested in …

2 Today was really tiring because …

3 I'm excited about …

4 … is boring because …

5 I think … is/are terrifying because …

6 I'm worried about …

I'm really interested in fashion.

6 **Work with a partner. Compare your sentences.**

A: I'm really interested in fashion.
B: I don't think fashion is very interesting. I'm really interested in music.

➡ **Vocabulary Bank • page 112**

Language focus 2 Quantifiers

1 **Complete the examples from the listening on page 66. Then complete the rules.**

1 There are ...*too many*... people. Look at the queue!

2 There's .... time to do everything. Don't worry about the queues.

3 How .... loops has it got?

4 We spent .... **much** money.

5 I'm hungry. **How** .... money have we got?

> 1 We use .... *much/many* to say an amount is excessive.
> 2 We use .... *much/many* to ask about quantity.
> 3 We use .... to say the amount is correct.

➡ **Grammar reference • page 104**

2 **Choose the correct words.**

1 There weren't **enough / much** rides.

2 We didn't go on everything. There were **too much / too many** rides.

3 **How much / How many** money did you spend at the park?

4 There weren't any shops and there weren't **many / much** restaurants either.

5 Did you have **enough / too many** time to go on all the rides?

a little / a few

3 **Complete the examples from the listening on page 66. Then choose the word to complete the rule.**

1 There are only .... people in the queue.

2 We've got .... time before the bus comes.

> We use *a little* and *a few* to express **big / small** quantities.

➡ **Grammar reference • page 104**

4 **Complete the sentences using *a few* or *a little*.**

1 We've got .... minutes before it opens.

2 There's .... pizza left. Do you want it?

3 Look! I took .... photos at the park.

4 I've only got .... pocket money.

5 We met .... friends at the park.

5 🔊 **2.18 Complete the conversation with the words in the box. Then listen and check.**

> too much a few how many enough
> a little how much (x2) too many ~~not much~~

A: Let's go on the roller coaster again.

B: I don't think so. There's [1] ...*not much*... time before the bus comes.

A: But it's so amazing!

B: [2] .... times do you want to go on it?

A: Well, OK, have we got [3] .... money to get a hot dog?

B: [4] .... are they?

A: They're £2 each.

B: Let's see. Yes, and we've got [5] .... extra money for something else!

A: Let's buy some more ice cream.

B: More? [6] .... ice cream can you eat?

A: I can never eat [7] .... ice cream!

B: I'm so tired. Let's sit down here for [8] .... minutes. I hope there aren't [9] .... people on the bus – I don't want to stand all the way home.

➡ **Say it right! • page 97**

Your turn

6 **Makes notes about the questions below.**

1 Have you ever been to a theme park? Did you like it?

2 Were there a lot of rides? Did you have enough time to go on all of them?

3 Were there a lot of people?

4 What rides were you afraid of at the park?

7 **Ask and answer with your partner about a theme park. Use your notes in Exercise 6 to help you.**

I went to a theme park called ... last summer. It was great.

Discover Culture

Mexico

1 **Work with a partner. Look at the photos and answer the questions.**

1 In which country is this ancient city?
2 Who lived there?
3 What is the chart do you think?
4 What is the connection with the sun and the moon?

Find out about the ancient Mayan calendar.

DISCOVERY
EDUCATION™ ▶

6.2 Calendars of the ancient Maya

2 ▶ **6.2** **Watch the first part of the video (to 1.14) and check your answers.**

3 ▶ **6.2** **Watch the first part of the video again and answer the questions.**

1 What question did the Maya think they could answer?
2 Why do scientists study the Mayan calendar?

4 ▶ **6.2** **Watch the next part of the video and complete the text.**

The calendar had 18 [1] .... of 20 days each, a total of [2] .... days.

Then there were five [3] .... days, a total of [4] .... days.

The calendar was very important. There are 365 [5] .... in the Kukulcan Temple: one for each day of the solar [6] ....

5 **Test your visual memory. Put these images in the correct order.**

a The Imix and Cimi symbols.
b The sun setting over a river.
c The moon passing above a palace.
d A view of a Mayan temple and beach.

6 **What do you remember about the calendar? Choose the correct word.**

Imix was a [1] **good / bad** day. They planned to do [2] **enjoyable / important** things, like planting on these days. Cimi was a [3] **good / bad** day. Its symbol was the [4] **closed / open** eye of a dead person. [5] **Everything / Nothing** important happened on these days.

7 ▶ **6.2** **Watch the whole video again and check your answers to Exercises 5 and 6.**

Your turn

8 **Work with a partner. Answer the questions.**

1 Do you think it's possible to predict good days and bad days? Why?/ Why not?
2 What's a good day for you? What's a bad day? Why? What kinds of things happen?

A: I think it's impossible, you never know what's going to happen.

B: I think the weather's important – if it's sunny, it could be a good day.

Superstitions?
Who needs them!

Superstitions have been around for thousands of years. A lot of people never walk under ladders or they believe that black cats bring **good** (or bad) luck. Some people think one magpie is bad luck but two together is good luck. Other superstitions are more modern, like football players who don't change their socks or who always enter the pitch with their right foot.

Lots of people, however, believe strongly that superstitions are **silly**. They say that superstitions are based on **old** habits, customs or beliefs. How could you have bad luck by opening an umbrella inside? Why is the number thirteen more **dangerous** than other numbers?

To prove their point, they have 'Anti-Superstition Parties', usually on Friday the thirteenth, a date that many people think brings bad luck. At these parties, people break mirrors and dance with open umbrellas. And nothing bad happens!

Peter Moore, a dentist, has been to several anti-superstition parties. He says, 'People must be crazy to believe that the number seven is **lucky** or that they could be more **successful** by putting a horseshoe outside their house.' Chelsea Evans, a chef, agrees. 'I love the parties. I've broken lots of mirrors and my life is going well!'

> **FACT!** *Fear of the number 13 is called Triskaidekaphobia and fear of Friday the Thirteenth is called Friggatriskaidekaphobia.*

Reading An article

1 Work with a partner. Look at the photos showing superstitions. What do you think the superstitions are?

2 🔊 **2.21** Read the article and check your answers.
Have you got the same superstitions in your country?

3 Read the article again. Are the sentences true or false? Correct the false ones.
1. All superstitions have a modern origin. *F*
2. Some superstitions come from modern beliefs.
3. Some football players wear two socks on one foot.
4. Anti-superstition parties are for people who believe in superstitions.
5. At anti-superstition parties, people don't follow any superstitions.
6. Peter and Chelsea are scared to go to anti-superstition parties.

Explore opposite adjectives

4 Look at the highlighted adjectives in the text. Match them to the opposite adjectives below.
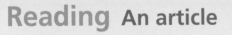
1. safe
2. unsuccessful
3. modern
4. unlucky
5. bad
6. sensible

➡ **Vocabulary Bank • page 112**

Your turn

5 Write about three superstitions in your country.

There are a lot of / a few / not many superstitions in my country. Some people believe/think/say that … are lucky.

6 Work with partner. Talk about the superstitions. Do you believe that people can create their own luck?

Speaking Expressing surprise

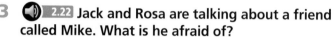

1 ▶ **6.3** **Watch the teenagers in the videos. How many teenagers …**

a) are afraid of animals?
b) say they are not afraid of anything?
c) are afraid of other things (not animals)?

2 💬 **What are *you* afraid of?**

3 🔊 **2.22** **Jack and Rosa are talking about a friend called Mike. What is he afraid of?**

4 **Complete the conversation with the useful language.**

5 🔊 **2.22** **Listen again and check your answers.**

6 💬 **Work with a partner. Practise the conversation in Exercise 4.**

7 💬 **Work with a partner. Prepare a conversation like the one in Exercise 4. Use the photos below and the useful language. Practise the conversation with your partner.**

Useful language

What?	I don't believe you/it!
That can't be true!	Are you serious?
You're joking!	No way!
That's impossible!	

Rosa: Is Mike going to come sailing with us?
Jack: No ¹ ..*way*.. ! He's terrified of deep water.
Rosa: ² .... ? That's ³ .... ! He's a really good swimmer!
Jack: No, it's true. He's got a phobia.
Rosa: That ⁴ .... true! He's competing in the 50 metre freestyle at the swimming club next week.
Jack: I know, but he's scared of swimming in open water. I think it's because you can't see the bottom.
Rosa: ⁵ .... serious? I didn't think Mike was scared of anything.
Jack: Well, he's afraid of deep water. It's quite a common phobia, actually.
Rosa: You're ⁶ .... ! I've never heard of it.
Jack: Mike told me himself.
Rosa: I don't ⁷ .... you! I'm going to call Mike and ask him.

Situation 1

You are going camping with some friends. Your friend Kevin has a phobia of spiders. He goes walking a lot, and loves sport.

Situation 2

You are going to go on a school trip to Rome. Your friend Donna is terrified of the dark. She is usually a confident person and speaks Italian!

✏️ Writing An email to a friend

1 Look at the photo and read Stefani's email. What is she worried about?

> **New mail +1** 📎
>
> Hi Pete,
>
> Thanks for the email with your news. My news is that I'm going to stay with my cousins in Norway this summer! I'm going with my parents and the idea is that we all go camping together. It's really exciting, but my problem is we're flying there! I've never been on a plane before and the truth is I'm really worried about flying. I don't know what to do! The fact is, when I think about flying over the sea, I feel tense and start sweating. It was embarrassing, but I had to tell my mum. She said it's just like going on a coach and told me not to worry. Not very helpful!
>
> What do you think?
>
> Regards,
>
> Stefani

2 Read Stefani's email again. Put the information she writes about in order.

- explain the problem
- open email and say thanks for Pete's news *1*
- write about who she has spoken to about it
- describe how she feels and why
- ask for advice and close email
- give news and explain her plans

Useful language

Introducing news and explaining things

We can use different phrases to introduce what we want to say.

- *My news is (that) …*
- *… the idea is (that) …*

3 Look at the Useful language box. Find two other examples of introducing something in the email.

4 Complete the sentences using the words in brackets.

1. We're moving to Germany. (our news) *Our news is that we're moving to Germany.*
2. We stay there for two years. (the idea)
3. She doesn't want to go. (the truth)
4. A lot of people have this phobia. (the fact)
5. They visit me next year. (the idea)
6. I've got a dog. (my big news)

✏️ Get writing

PLAN

5 Plan an email to a friend with your news and explaining a problem you have. Make notes on the things in Exercise 2.

WRITE

6 Write your email. Use your notes from Exercise 5 and the model text to help you.

CHECK

7 Can you say YES to these questions?

- Is the information from Exercise 2 in your email?
- Have you used expressions like *My news is that …* in your email?

71

Vocabulary

1 Match the communication words with the comments.

> blog post   Tweet   forum   Skype™
> social media post   ~~text message~~

1 I can send short messages and it's cheaper than a phone call.   *text message*
2 I can chat with my friends and see them at the same time.
3 I can send really short messages to all my friends at the same time.
4 I can add photos and videos and my friends can visit my page.
5 I can ask questions and post messages and anyone on the list can reply.
6 I can write about my life and the things I'm interested in and anyone can read it.

2 Match the words with the definitions.

1 whisper   *c*   5 complain
2 boast   6 joke
3 criticise   7 shout
4 argue

a to say something is wrong
b to speak angrily with someone
c to talk very quietly
d to talk very loudly
e to say something funny
f to speak too proudly about something you have done
g to give a bad opinion about something

3 Match the sentences to the fears in the box.

> birds   clowns   lifts   ~~flying~~   the dark   snakes

1 I prefer taking the bus or train.   *flying*
2 I'll take the stairs.
3 I don't like them flying near me.
4 They can be poisonous and they move quickly.
5 They look frightening with their face and hair different colours.
6 Can you leave the light on?

4 Complete the sentences with the correct adjective form of the words in brackets.

1 Matthew feels really _tired_ (tire).
2 Their new computer game is really .... (excite).
3 The TV programme was so .... (bore). I fell asleep.
4 Jason saw a spider and he was really .... (terrify).
5 Harry's book is really .... (interest).
6 Julie's test is tomorrow. She feels very .... (worry).

Explore vocabulary

5 Complete the text with the words in the box. Use the correct form of the phrasal verbs.

> virtual friends   come into use   get by
> ~~social network sites~~   turn into   face-to-face
> digital generation   personal information

The number of people using ¹_social network sites_ is going up along with the number of ² .... that they have. In the past, we ³ .... with telephones and letters but the current ⁴ .... have access to different ways of communicating. Since computers, tablets and mobile phones have ⁵ ...., we have less ⁶ .... contact with friends and family and instead we prefer to give ⁷ .... for everyone to read. Are we ⁸ .... a generation of people who can't communicate with each other without a gadget?

6 Complete the sentences with *of, about* or *with*. Then write the opposite adjective of the underlined words.

1 Is that lift <u>safe</u>? I'm terrified _of_ small spaces.   *dangerous*
2 What do you think .... this <u>old</u> mobile phone? It's enormous!
3 A: Ana won't share her <u>lucky</u> objects .... me.
   B: Well, you should find your own lucky things!
4 I'm really worried .... the exam. I saw a black cat too and that's <u>bad</u> luck!
5 A: Are you dressing up for the party?
   B: No, I'm embarrassed .... looking <u>silly</u>.

Language focus

1 Complete the sentences about life in the year 2050. Use *will*, *won't* or *might/may not*.

1 Everyone ..*will*.. use the Internet for shopping, I'm sure.
2 I think some schools .... offer classes on Skype™.
3 Cars .... use petrol, I'm sure. They'll be electric.
4 Lots of people .... probably work from home.
5 Robots .... definitely do all the housework – at least I hope so!
6 It's possible we .... read books anymore.

2 Complete the first conditional sentences. Use the verbs in brackets.

1 The librarian ..*will be*.. (be) upset if we ..*talk*.. (talk) too loudly in the library.
2 If you .... (not answer) my email, I .... (not write) to you ever again!
3 If we .... (get) Skype™, we .... (not pay) so much for our phone calls.
4 You .... (might win) the lottery if you .... (buy) a ticket.
5 You .... (not find out) what's happening in the world if you .... (not use) the Internet.
6 If she .... (have) her mobile with her, her mum .... (not worry) about her.
7 He .... (send) you a text message if he .... (hear) any news.
8 If he .... (work) hard enough, he .... (might win) a prize.

3 Complete the sentences with *be going to*, *will* or present continuous.

1 He ..*is flying*.. (fly) to Japan tomorrow.
2 Don't worry. He .... probably .... (call) you later.
3 My parents .... (take) me out for dinner on Saturday for my birthday.
4 What .... (you/do) when you leave school?
5 Sorry, but we .... (not see) you later – we have got a party to go to.
6 Susan .... (start) a new job on Monday.

4 Choose the correct words.

I had a terrible time at the concert last weekend. There were ¹ **too much / (too many)** people and there was ² **too much / too many** noise. There wasn't ³ **enough / a few** space in the hall and I felt quite scared. There were only ⁴ **a few / a little** windows and they were closed. I felt sick and I needed ⁵ **a few / a little** time to sit down and recover. There weren't ⁶ **too many / enough** chairs to sit on so luckily ⁷ **a few / too many** friends helped me. One friend asked me, '⁸ **How many / How much** concerts have you been to?' 'Lots!' I told her.

Language builder

5 Choose the correct words to complete the text.

Wish you were here!

Lisa:	Hi, Mike! I haven't seen you ¹ *a* ages!
Mike:	I know! I ² .... on a trip to New York City and I ³ .... back. ⁴ .... been there?
Lisa:	No, I don't like big cities. There are usually ⁵ .... people and there's ⁶ .... noise.
Mike:	I love New York! If you ⁷ .... around the city you ⁸ .... some great places to eat and things to see. And I went to ⁹ .... jazz concerts, too.
Lisa:	Where ¹⁰ .... next?
Mike:	I'm not sure, I ¹¹ .... to Beijing and Shanghai.
Lisa:	That sounds great. If you go ¹² .... let me know?
Mike:	Sure!

	a	b	c
1	for	since	some
2	was going	have gone	went
3	was just coming	have just come	came just
4	Have you ever	Did you ever	Were you ever
5	too much	too many	a few
6	too much	too many	a little
7	walked	walk	have walked
8	find	are finding	will find
9	a little	a few	enough
10	you will visit	are you visiting	are you going to visit
11	might go	will go	'm going
12	I will	you will	will you

Speaking

6 Match the sentences.

1 You don't need to worry. *d*
2 That can't be true!
3 Listen, I think I can help you.
4 Are you serious?
5 Of course you can do it.
6 I don't believe you!

a Well, why don't you ask him.
b Thanks, but I'm really worried.
c Yes, she's afraid of spiders.
d I know, you're right.
e Thanks, I feel more confident now.
f I know, but it is.

7 School life

Discovery EDUCATION

In this unit ...

The women of
Ayoquesco **p77**

Playing with
Maths **p80**

Asking for advice **p82**

CLIL Social
media **p121**

Vocabulary
- Behaviour and discipline
  at school
- Words from the text
- *make* and *do*
- Phrasal verbs

Language focus
- Second conditional:
  affirmative and negative
  statements, *yes/no*
  questions
- Second conditional:
  Wh- questions

Unit aims
I can ...
- talk about behaviour and discipline
  at school.
- talk about imaginary situations.
- ask questions about imaginary situations.
- understand an article about teaching in
  Singapore.
- ask for and give advice.
- write a problem page.

BE CURIOUS

What can you see in the photo?
Start thinking
- What are the children doing?
- How important is your
  working environment at
  school?
- What are the best and worst
  parts of going to school?

Vocabulary Life at school

1 🔊 **2.23** Match the words and phrases in the box with the photos (a–i). Then listen, check and repeat.

> bullying   hand in homework   get detention   ~~cheat in a test~~   be on time
> wear a uniform   write lines   scream or shout   get good marks

a   *cheat in a test*

2 Look again at the phrases in Exercise 1. Which are bad or good behaviours and which are rules or punishments?

3 🔊 **2.24** Listen to the conversation between David from the UK and Anita from Brazil about schools. Which things from Exercise 1 do they talk about?

Your turn

4 Work with a partner. Answer the questions.
1   Do you wear a uniform in your school? Why/Why not?
2   What do you think of cheating in tests?
3   Do you think your school is strict? Why/Why not?

We don't have to wear a uniform because …

I think cheating is bad because …

Our school is very strict because we always have to …

➡ **Vocabulary Bank • page 113**

Reading A student blog

1 **Work with a partner. Look at the photo and answer the questions.**

1 Where are the children?

2 Who are they?

3 What do you think they're discussing?

2 🔊 **2.25** **Read the article about a school in New York. In what ways is it different from other schools?**

3 **Read the article again. Are the sentences true or false? Correct the false ones.**

1 The school has meetings every month. *F*

2 The students make suggestions and the teachers vote on their suggestions.

3 There are no rules.

4 The students can't choose their own subjects.

5 The teachers don't tell the students what to do.

6 Working in a team is very important at the Free School.

👁 Get it right!

We use the infinitive after **want**.
*If you want **to talk**, you have to put up your hand.*
*I don't want **to do** the exam tomorrow!*

Explore words in context

4 **Match the words and phrases from the article with the definitions (1–5) below.**

> propose   vote   walk out   on our own together

1 decide

2 alone – without other people

3 the opposite of alone

4 make a suggestion

5 leave a room without asking for permission

Your turn

5 **Answer the questions. Make notes.**

1 Would you like to go to a school like the Brooklyn Free School? Why/Why not?

2 What rules would you change in your school? Why?

3 What subjects would you like to study that you don't already study? Why?

6 **Discuss your answers in groups.**

I'd really like/love/hate to go to a school like this.
I'd like to change the rule about ... because it's ...
I'd really like to study .... I think it's important/ interesting because ...

BROWN'S FREE SCHOOL ✕

This week's student blogger is a new student, Jacklyn Whyte.

A lot of people are asking me about my new school. It's really hard to explain, so I give them an example of one day.

It's Wednesday morning and it's time for the weekly school meeting. This week, one of the topics is 'wheels'. Kyle, one of the kids in my class, proposes a new rule that students can bring skateboards, skates and bicycles to school. Our teacher, Mr Jackson, suggests that we do this one day a week and the whole school votes on a 'wheels' day for next Friday.

If I wanted to change the rules at my old school, it wouldn't be that easy! But here at the Brown's Free School, things are different. Here, *we* make the decisions! We can decide to go to class, watch TV or play a computer game, but most students choose to go to class – it's more interesting! When we don't like a class, we just walk out! In my old school, if I didn't stay until the end of a class, I'd be in detention!

At the Free School, the teachers don't give detention, and no one writes lines. There's no uniform and there are no exams. We choose what we want to study and how. We can work in groups, or study on our own. If you were at the school and you wanted to study car mechanics, our teachers would help you find a way to study it. If you wanted to start a new school magazine, you would suggest it to the teachers. Then, they would find a way to help you do it.

That's how the Free School works. The ideas come from the students and everyone works together to make them happen. It's a great experience and I love going to the Free School!

add a comment | send a message

FACT! *Although the USA has the most free schools in the world, many other countries have free schools too, including Brazil, India, Japan, the UK and Germany.*

Language focus 1 Second conditional

1 Complete the examples from the text on page 76. Then complete the rules.

imaginary situation	possible consequence
If I …. …. until the end of a class,	I …. …. in detention!
If you …. to start a new school magazine,	you …. …. it to the teachers.

1 We use …. + past simple and …. + infinitive to form the second conditional.
2 We use the second conditional to talk about unreal situations in the present or **future / past**.

 Grammar reference • page 105

2 Look at the chart. Choose the correct form of the verbs in the sentences below.

1 If I (was) / 'd be rude to a teacher, I got / ('d get) detention.
2 If I **didn't / wouldn't** pass my exams, my parents **didn't / wouldn't** be very happy!
3 If a teacher **gave / would give** me lines, I **wrote / 'd write** them during the break.
4 My teacher **called / would call** my parents if I **didn't / wouldn't** go to school.
5 My friends **did / would** like to go to the Free School if they **opened / would open** one in our town.
6 I **didn't / wouldn't** study Maths if I **went / would go** to the Free School.

3 Write complete sentences.

1 If I / go / to the Free School / not study Maths
   If I went to the Free School, I wouldn't study Maths.
2 If I / not do homework / my teacher / give / detention
3 If I / not study English / not know / how to do this exercise
4 I / tell / my parents / if / there / be / bullying in my school
5 I / do / art in class / if / have the choice
6 I / not get / good marks / if / not study every day

 **Say it right!** • page 97

Your turn

4 Read the quiz and choose answers for you.

> **1 If I came home late one night, …**
> a my parents would be very angry.
> b my parents wouldn't say anything.
> c I'd get some kind of punishment.
>
> **2 If I was rude to one of my parents, …**
> a I'd feel bad and I'd say sorry immediately.
> b they'd be very shocked because I'm never rude.
> c they'd punish me with no TV or computer for a week.
>
> **3 If I borrowed something from my brother/sister/ friend without asking, …**
> a it wouldn't be a problem. They do it to me all the time!
> b they'd tell my parents and I'd get into a lot of trouble!
> c I'd put it back before they noticed.

5 Compare your quiz answers with your partner.

If I came home late, I'd get some kind of punishment. I wouldn't go out for two or three weeks.

Learn about a successful business.
● What happened in Ayoquezco in 1979?
● What do people use prickly pear for?
● What did the women decide to do?

7.1 The women of Ayoquezco

Listening A discussion

1 🔊 `2.28` **Listen to the quiz. Put the pictures in the correct order.**

2 🔊 `2.28` **Listen again and choose the correct answers.**

1 If Mick saw a classmate cheating in an exam, he would …
 a say nothing and just continue with his work.
 b tell a teacher.
 c try to cheat as well.

2 If Suzy found a wallet full of money on the street near her school, she would …
 a take it to the nearest police station.
 b give it to a teacher at the school.
 c keep it.

3 What is Mick more careful about now?
 a Not losing his mobile phone.
 b What he tells his dad.
 c Who he gives his phone number to.

4 If someone sent Suzy some horrible messages on her phone she would …
 a show them to her parents.
 b do nothing.
 c tell the police.

3 **Work with a partner. Discuss what you would do in the situations in Exercise 3.**

Vocabulary *make* and *do*

4 🔊 `2.29` **Match the words in the box to the verbs, *make* or *do*. Then listen, check and repeat.**

> ~~your homework~~   ~~a mistake~~   friends   a noise
> an exercise   a phone call   something interesting
> a mess   the right thing   decision

do your homework ….
make a mistake ….

➡️ **Vocabulary Bank • page 113**

Your turn

5 **Complete the questions with the correct verb *make* or *do* then answer the questions. Make notes.**

1 Do you find it easy to …. friends?
2 How many hours of homework do you …. every week?
3 How do you feel when you …. a mistake in class?
4 Does your mum get angry with you when you …. a mess in your room?

6 **Ask and answer with your partner.**

I find it easy to make friends because I'm not very shy.

Language focus 2 Second conditional questions

1 **Complete the examples from the listening on page 78.**

Wh- questions
What **would** you do **if** you saw someone cheating? **If** you found a wallet, what .... you do?

Yes/No questions	Short answers
.... someone **sent** you horrible messages on your phone would you tell a teacher? **Would** you tell your parents **if** you **failed** an exam?	Yes, I/you/he/she/it/we/they would. No, I/you/he/she/it/we/they wouldn't.

➡ **Grammar reference • page 105**

2 **Look at the chart. Choose the correct words to complete the sentences.**

1 What **did** / **would** you do if you **were** / **would be** the head teacher of your school?
2 If your best friend **didn't** / **wouldn't** invite you to his/her birthday, what **did** / **would** you say?
3 If your family **lived** / **would live** in an English-speaking country, **did** / **would** your lives be very different?
4 What job **did** / **would** your teacher do if he/she **wasn't** / **wouldn't be** a teacher?
5 If your grandparents **lived** / **would live** in the USA, **did** / **would** you go to visit them?

3 🔊 **2.30** **Complete the conversation with the correct form of the verbs in brackets. Then listen and check.**

A: Can I ask you a few questions?
B: Yes, sure.
A: OK, first question: what [1] _would_ you .... (do) if you [2] .... (win) a TV talent show?
B: Wow! I think I'd have a huge party with all my friends and family!
A: And if you [3] .... (have) a party, where [4] .... you .... (have) it?
B: I'd definitely have it on a beach, if I could!
A: OK, second question. If you [5] .... (can) be famous, what [6] .... you .... (be)?
B: I don't know. I'd like to be a singer maybe.
A: OK. Last question. If you [7] .... (not have to) go to school, what [8] .... you .... (do) all day?
B: That's easy! I'd play my guitar, listen to music and spend time with my friends!
A: Thank you!

Your turn

4 **Answer the questions. Make notes.**

1 If you had a million pounds, what would you buy?
2 If you ruled the world, what would you change?
3 If you didn't have to go to school, what would you do all day?
4 If you could learn a musical instrument, which instrument would you learn?
5 If you weren't a teenager, what age would you like to be?
6 If you were 18, what would you do that you can't do now?

5 **Ask and answer the questions in Exercise 4 with your partner.**
Let me think. OK, if I had a million pounds, I'd buy a really big house by the sea!

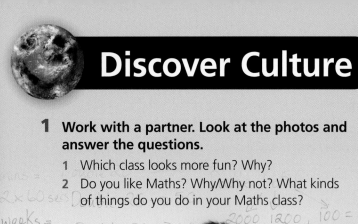

Discover Culture

1 **Work with a partner. Look at the photos and answer the questions.**

1 Which class looks more fun? Why?
2 Do you like Maths? Why/Why not? What kinds of things do you do in your Maths class?

Find out about learning Maths.

⦿DISCOVERY EDUCATION™ ⊙

7.2 Playing with Maths

2 ⊙ 7.2 **Watch the video without sound. Try to answer the questions.**

1 How do we use Maths in everyday life?
2 What is the first group of pupils learning about? (0.27–1.09)
3 What is the second group of pupils learning about? (1.10–2.30)

3 ⊙ 7.2 **Watch the video with sound and check your answers.**

4 ⊙ 7.2 **Watch the video with sound and complete the sentences.**

1 Students either love or .... Maths.
2 We use Maths to measure distance, design art work, go shopping and .....
3 Students get into groups to learn about ....
4 Students do .... to learn about shapes in Maths.
5 The students find geometric shapes in different ....
6 Learning Maths this way is interesting and ....

5 **Test your visual memory about what the students do. Are these statements true or false? If false, correct them.**

1 There is a student running in a race at the start.
2 The first groups of students do the fractions game in pairs.
3 The students in the Art/Maths class sit on chairs in front of the teacher.
4 The students have to discover geometry in art.
5 They write down a list of the different shapes on the board.

6 **What objects do you see in the video? How is each one used in the Maths class?**

> marbles ~~a mouse (computer)~~ smartphone
> a quilt a clock small stones a football

a mouse – we use Maths when we use a computer

Your turn

7 **Ask and answer with your partner.**

1 Which of the two Maths lessons in the video do you like the most? Why?
2 When do you use Maths outside class? Do your classes help with these things? Why/Why not?

I use Maths when I ...
We don't need maths class for everyday life, we have calculators.

Reading An article

1 Work with a partner. Look at the photo of Singapore and make a list of at least three adjectives to describe the city.

2 🔊 **2.31** Read the article about Singapore. What's the main focus of the article?

a The location and geography of the country
b Learning languages in Singapore
c A new way of teaching an old subject

3 Read the article again and answer the questions.

1 Where is Singapore?
2 What is special about the country?
3 Is the Singapore approach to teaching Maths a traditional Asian approach?
4 At what age do children start school in Singapore?
5 How do children learn basic ideas in Maths in Singapore?
6 Which countries have adopted the Singapore approach?

Explore phrasal verbs

4 Look at the highlighted words in the text. Match the phrasal verbs in the box with the definitions (1–5).

> pick up   find out   write out   work out   try out

1 write something again more completely
2 do the calculation to find an answer to Maths problem
3 learn something new
4 test something to see if it works
5 get information about something or learn about it

➡ **Vocabulary Bank • page 113**

Your turn

5 Compare the primary school with yours. Write sentences. Compare your sentences with your partner.

	classroom atmosphere	learning things
Singapore		
My school		

Singapore
A SUCCESS STORY

Singapore is a fascinating place. It's a giant floating city 130 kilometres north of the Equator. The city has four official languages – Chinese, Malay, Tamil and English. English is the language everyone uses for official business and all the schools teach English.

Singapore is one of the smallest countries in the world, but it is also one of the richest. For years, it has been famous for its high level of education – and it's the number one country in the world for teaching Maths. Most people think that Asian schools in general are very strict. Is this the secret of Singapore's great success too? Not at all! If you walked into a Maths class in a primary school in Singapore, you'd be surprised by how active and noisy it was. You wouldn't see children sitting quietly in their chairs watching their teacher at the board and **writing out** sums in their notebooks. You would see a lot of activity and hear a lot of noise.

School starts at the age of seven in Singapore. The Maths programme starts very slowly and the younger children spend a lot of time on the first steps. They use everyday objects, like beans and fruit, to feel and see the basic ideas. They don't copy from the board or do exercises in their books – they **pick** Maths **up** through playing. By sharing objects with friends, they **find out** about division. By building towers with blocks, they learn addition. It looks like the children are simply playing, but they're not – they're **working out** the answers to complex problems in a fun and interesting way.

Would this system work if it was taught in your country? A lot of schools around the world have **tried** it **out** – the UK for example, and the USA. And it's been a great success.

> **FACT!** The largest Maths class was given in Nigeria in July 2013 with 2,381 people in the class.

Speaking Asking for and giving advice

1 ▶ **7.3** Watch the teenagers in the video. How many teenagers …

a) would talk to a member of their family?
b) would talk to a friend?
c) say they would get good advice?

2 💬 Who would *you* talk to if you needed advice?

3 🔊 **2.32** Hayley is talking to her friend James. What does Hayley want advice about?

4 Complete the conversation with the useful language.

Useful language

What's the problem?
I need your advice.
It's a good idea to …
What do you think I should do?
If I were you I wouldn't …
Maybe we could …
Have you tried …?
They say I shouldn't worry.

Hayley: James, can I talk to you? I ¹ *need your* advice.
James: Yes, of course. What's ² …. ?
Hayley: Well, there's a girl in my class who is saying nasty things about me.
James: Really? What sort of things?
Hayley: Oh, that I copy her homework and cheat in exams. It's awful! What do you think ³ …. do?
James: Look, if I were you, I ⁴ …. listen to her. What do your other friends say?
Hayley: They say I ⁵ …. worry. But I can't help it.
James: Yeah. Perhaps it's ⁶ …. idea to do something.
Hayley: Yes, but what?
James: Well, have you ⁷ …. talking to her? Maybe we ⁸ …. do it together.
Hayley: Yes, that's a good idea. Thanks, James!

5 🔊 **2.32** Listen again and check your answers.

6 💬 Work with a partner. Practise the conversation in Exercise 4.

7 💬 Work with a partner. Prepare a conversation like the one in Exercise 4. Use the photos below and the useful language. Practise the conversation with your partner.

Problem 1

Someone in your class has taken your mobile phone. (nobody knows who)

Problem 2

You have lost two text books you left in the classroom yesterday.

Writing A problem page

1 Read Paula's letter. What is the problem?

| FRIENDS | SCHOOL | HOMEWORK | FAMILY |

My English teacher hates me!

Paula asked 4 days ago

Hi everyone

I need some advice. I think my teacher hates me. I've had detention every week for the last four weeks from Mr Harris, my English teacher. English was always my best subject and Mr Harris was my favourite teacher, but now I'm not getting good marks. He's always giving me detention. What should I do?

best answer

LiverpoolLad answered 2 days ago

I think maybe the problem is not only your teacher but also your marks. You say that English was your best subject and that your marks haven't been very good recently. Perhaps your English teacher is strict because he wants to show you that he's not happy with your marks. It's possible that he's trying to make you work harder by giving you detention.

I think you should try talking to him because communication is always the best way to work out a solution to a problem. You should ask him what the problem is and why you are getting detention. You could also work harder to improve your marks.

I really hope this helps.

2 Read the answer from LiverpoolLad again. What things does he do in his answer?

- Give a title
- Say what he thinks the real problem might be
- Give reasons for his opinions
- Offer different ways of looking at the problem
- Give direct orders
- Offer several solutions
- Give reasons for his advice
- Write a final sentence to make the person feel better

Summarising a problem and giving advice
Use different phrases to summarise what you want to say and to give advice.
- *I think maybe the problem is not only … but also …*
- *You say that …*
- *I think you should try … because …*

3 Look at the Useful language box. Find two other phrases to give advice in Exercise 1.

4 Complete the sentences with the words in the box.

| should try problem possible Perhaps also |

1 I think maybe the .... is your marks. .... your teacher is angry with you. It's .... that he wants to encourage you.
2 You .... talk to him. I think you should .... asking him for advice. You could .... study harder.

 Get writing

PLAN

5 Read the problem below. Plan your answer. Make notes on the things in Exercise 2.

> Isabel cheated in a Maths test. It was the first time and she feels bad. She didn't study and she wrote the answers on her arm. She got a good mark and her parents are going to buy her a new mobile.

WRITE

6 Write your answer. Use your notes from Exercise 5 and the model text to help you.

CHECK

7 Can you say YES to these questions?
- Is the information from the plan in your answer?
- Have you used different expressions to restate the problem and to give your advice?

8 Green planet

In this unit ...

Where does it all go? **p87**

Build it better **p90**

Doing voluntary work **p92**

CLIL Driving into the future **p122**

Vocabulary
- Materials
- Words from the text
- Energy issues
- Phrasal verbs

Language focus
- Present simple passive
- Past simple passive

Unit aims
I can ...
- talk about types of materials.
- describe how materials are recycled.
- talk about the energy I use at home.
- understand a text about renewable energy.
- apologise and explain to a friend.
- write a newspaper article.

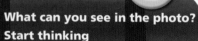

BE CURIOUS

What can you see in the photo?
Start thinking
- What is a wind farm?
- What do wind turbines produce?
- Why are they good for the environment?

Vocabulary Materials

1 🔊 **2.33** Match a material (or materials) in the box with objects in the photos. Then listen, check and repeat. What's the function of each of the objects?

> bricks   cement   cotton   glass   leather   metal   paper   plastic   rubber   ~~wood~~

a   *wood*

2 Match the materials from Exercise 1 with the sentences.
1   We often use this material to make furniture like chairs and tables. *wood*
2   We often use this material to make shoes, bags, and belts.
3   If you drop a bottle made of this material, it will probably break.
4   This material is very common for making T-shirts.
5   We make tyres for cars with this material.
6   This is the most common material used to make books.
7   These two materials are very common for building houses.

> **◉ Get it right!**
> We don't use **the** before plural nouns to talk about things in a general way. ✓
> *We often use this material to make ~~the~~ shoes.* ✗

3 🔊 **2.34** Listen to the conversation. Complete the chart with the things they talk about.

leather	*shoes*
cotton	
glass	
wood	
paper	
rubber	
plastic	
metal	

Your turn

4 Think of two objects you've got at home for each of the materials in Exercise 1. Make notes. Work with a partner. Tell him/her about the objects.

I've got a lot of leather shoes.

➲ **Vocabulary Bank** • page 114

➲ **Say it right!** • page 97

Reading An article

1 Work with a partner. Look at the pictures and answer the questions.

  1 What are the people building?
  2 What materials are they using?
  3 Why are they using them?

2 🔊 **2.37** Read an article about Mike Reynolds. What kind of houses does he build?

3 Read the article again and answer the questions.

  1 How does Mike protect his Earthships from the cold?
  2 How does he provide light during the day?
  3 Why does he grow his plants in the front of the house?
  4 How does he get energy and water?
  5 How did he and his organisation help other people?
  6 What is Mike's main message to the world?

Explore words in context

4 Match the verbs in the box with the definitions (1–7).

> warrior throw away shaped match
> decoration northern reuse

  1 made into a particular form or shape
  2 use again
  3 someone who fights for something
  4 be similar to or look the same
  5 put something in the rubbish
  6 things used to make something look beautiful
  7 from the north

Your turn

5 Which materials do you recycle or reuse at school or at home? What do you do with them? Makes notes.

6 Talk about your notes from Exercise 5. Is it easy to recycle materials in your area? Why/Why not?

  At school, we recycle some of our rubbish.

  My mum takes plastic stuff to a special container.

  It's very easy to recycle materials where I live. There's a container for every type of rubbish.

GARBAGE WARRIOR

Mike Reynolds builds houses from recycled materials.

Mike Reynolds builds houses from recycled materials to show us what we waste. Mike's houses are built using the things that other people throw away. His Earthships (as his houses are called) are beautiful buildings. They are shaped and coloured to match the landscape around them. He uses bottles to create beautiful walls full of light. There are plants everywhere, inside and out. But the plants and the bottles, like everything else in the Earthships, are not only there for decoration. Every single material in an Earthship is carefully chosen. Old car tyres are used to build strong walls. The rubber protects the houses from the cold northern winds in winter. These walls are built at the back of the house. The walls at the front of the house are built from metal cans or glass bottles. They're held together with the earth from around them and cement is not used at all. The beautiful bottle walls are built to the south to give light during the day. The house is heated by the larger front windows. They also create the perfect temperature for growing all kinds of fruit and vegetables, and the plants are protected against the bad weather. When you live in an Earthship, you grow your own food, get electricity from the sun and wind and you get water from the rain and snow.

Mike and the Earthship organisation use their ability and experience to help people all over the world. In 2010, they visited victims of the earthquake in Haiti. They taught them how to build safe, new homes quickly and cheaply from materials that they could find around them. Mike points out that rubbish only exists because we humans create it. That is exactly what Mike, the Garbage Warrior, wants us to see – that we have to stop waste and reuse our rubbish.

> **FACT!** Recycled tyres are used to build roads and pavements.

An Earthship home. These houses are a symbol of his fight against waste.

Language focus 1 Present simple passive

1 **Complete the examples from the text on page 86. Then complete the rules.**

+	Old car tyres …. …. to build walls. The house …. …. by the larger front windows.
–	Cement …. …. . Mike's houses **are not built** with traditional materials.

1 To form the passive, use …. + past participle.
2 Active: They make the houses from rubbish.
3 Passive: The houses …. from rubbish.

→ **Grammar reference • page 106**

2 **Look at the chart. Complete the sentences. Use the passive form of the verbs in brackets.**

1 The house (make) of bottles and cans.
   The house is made of bottles and cans.
2 The cans (recycle) to build walls.
3 The walls (design) to protect the house from extreme temperatures.
4 The heat from the sun (use) to give power to the house.
5 The water from the kitchen (reuse) in the garden.
6 The houses (build) into the side of a hill.

3 **🔊 2.38 Choose the correct words to complete the text. Then listen and check.**

Rows and rows of human statues are standing in the main square. As you [1] **move / are moved** closer, you [2] **see / are seen** that they [3] **make / are made** of all kinds of everyday objects. Some [4] **build / are built** from plastic bags, bottles and cans. Others [5] **decorate / are decorated** with computer keyboards or TV screens. The Trash Army, as it [6] **call / is called**, is a travelling exhibition. It has travelled all over the world and it [7] **shows / is shown** people how much rubbish we [8] **produce / is produced** through our modern lifestyles.

Present simple passive questions

4 **Look at the questions about the text on page 86 and complete the rule.**

● Are the walls in Mike's house **made** of bricks?
● Why **are** rubber tyres **used**?
● What **are** the walls at the front of the house **made** from?
● Is the house **heated** by electricity?

To form questions we use …. + subject + …. .

5 **Answer the questions in Exercise 4 about the text.**

6 **Order the questions.**

1 your / wood / house / is / made of?
2 recycled / the plastic bottles / your / are / in / house?
3 for / later / newspapers and magazines / old / are / saved?
4 reused / plastic bags / are?
5 your / vegetables / are / grown / garden / in?

Your turn

7 **Ask and answer the questions in Exercise 6.**
A: Is your house made of wood?
B: No, it isn't. It's made of bricks.

A bathroom

Learn about rubbish in the sea.
● What sort of rubbish do you think is found in the sea?
● Why is the sea so important for the planet?
● What happens to rubbish in the sea?

●Discovery EDUCATION™

8.1 **Where does it all go?**

Listening A class presentation

1 Work with a partner. Look at the picture of a living room and say how the room is similar to and different from the living room in your home.

2 🔊 **2.39** The living room is an exhibit in a museum. Listen to three students talking about the house. What do they talk about?

a Heating homes in the past
b Changing technology at home
c Energy at home

3 🔊 **2.39** Listen again and answer the questions.

1 How long has the Eco House been open?
2 What does the museum use the Eco House for?
3 What does Rebecca say about computers?
4 What uses the most energy?
5 What did the experiment show?
6 What does the last student want to discuss about the house?

Vocabulary Energy issues

4 Match the verbs from the class presentation with the definitions (1–7).

> consume   leave on standby   switch off   waste
> save energy   turn down   reduce

1 to use energy
2 to stop energy being wasted
3 to use more energy than you need
4 to make something smaller
5 to leave an appliance connected to the electricity
6 to disconnect an appliance from the electricity
7 you use less energy by doing this with an appliance

5 🔊 **2.40** Complete the sentences with the correct form of the verbs in Exercise 4. Then listen and check.

1 Don't forget to ...*switch off*... the lights before you go to bed.
2 Can you .... the heating? It's really warm.
3 You shouldn't .... the TV .... at night.
4 Did you know your computer .... a lot of electricity?
5 It's better to have a shower than a bath because you don't .... so much water.
6 You should try to .... the number of hours you use the air conditioning.
7 We're trying to .... so I always switch off my computer when I'm not using it.

Your turn

6 Ask and answer with your partner.

1 How do you save energy in your house?
2 How do you think you could save more energy at home?
3 Why is it important to save energy?

I always switch of my computer and the monitor before I go to bed.

I leave the TV on standby so I should switch it off.

Saving energy is important for the environment.

➔ **Vocabulary Bank • page 114**

Language focus 2

Past simple passive

1 Complete the examples from the listening on page 88.

+	The Eco house …. **built** in 1985. Several changes …. **made** to the house.
–	A lot of rubbish …. **recycled** in the 1980s. The lights **were not** switched off for a week.
with by	The Eco house **was designed by** the museum.

➔ Grammar reference • page 106

2 Complete the sentences. Use the past simple passive form of the verbs in brackets.

1 The Eco house …*was completed*… (complete) in 1985.
2 It …. (build) on a large piece of land.
3 A lot of energy …. (save) by turning down the temperature.
4 The kitchen …. (redesign) two years ago.
5 A lot of changes …. (make) to the house.
6 The old fridge and washing machine …. (not throw) away.

3 Write the active sentences below using the past passive and *by*.

1 Companies first used plastic bottles in 1947.
Plastic bottles were first used in 1947.
2 They finished the Burj Al Arab hotel in Dubai in 1999.
3 The Chinese invented paper almost 2,000 years ago.
4 Europeans threw out about 100 million mobile phones last year.
5 Swiss people recycled 96% of glass bottles in 2012.
6 John Dunlop made the first rubber tyre for his son's bicycle.

Past simple passive questions

4 Complete the examples from the listening on page 88.

Wh- questions
Why …. the Eco house …. ? When **was** the house **completed**?
Yes/No questions and short answers
…. a lot of energy …. by reducing the temperature? Yes, it **was**./No, it **wasn't**. **Were** the lights **switched** off last night? Yes, they **were**./No, they **weren't**.

➔ Grammar reference • page 106

5 🔊 2.41 Complete the conversation with the correct form of the past simple passive. Then listen and check.

> **A:** Hey, shall we do this general knowledge quiz?
> **B:** OK. But I'm not very good!
> **A:** OK, first question. [1]…. *Don Quixote* [2]…. (write) by Shakespeare?
> **B:** That's easy! No, it [3]….. It [4]…. by Cervantes.
> **A:** Good! Question two – [5]…. the first modern Olympic Games [6]…. (hold) in Greece?
> **B:** No, they [7]….. They [8]…. in London.
> **A:** No, it was Athens! OK, the last question – again it's very easy! Who [9]…. Harry Potter [10]…. (play) by?
> **B:** I know that one! He [11]…. by Daniel Radcliffe – easy!

> **Your turn**

6 Write five general knowledge quiz questions using the past passive. Use the questions in Exercises 5 and 6 to help.

In the Spider Man films, who was Spider Man's girlfriend played by?

7 Ask and answer your questions with your partner. Give full sentences.

A: In the Spider Man films, who was Spider Man's girlfriend played by?
B: She was played by Emma Stone.

Discover Culture

1 Work with a partner. Look at the photos and describe them. What do you think the video will be about?

North America

Find out about building sustainably.

⚫ Discovery EDUCATION™

8.2 Build it better

2 ▶ **8.2** Watch the video without sound and check your ideas.

3 Which of the words below do you think you will hear in the video?

> tornado   flood   sustainable   renewable
> sunlight   rain   mirror   solar panels   natural
> electricity   environment

4 ▶ **8.2** Watch the video with sound. Check your answers to Exercise 3.

5 ▶ **8.2** Watch the video again and match the information.

1	hail stones	a	of homes and businesses destroyed
2	95%	b	Greensburg was created
3	the wind speed was	c	create energy for the building
4	the solar panels	d	the size of tennis balls
5	a new and improved	e	320 km per hour

6 Complete the text about rebuilding Greensburg. Use the words in the box.

> mirror   holes   solar panels   tubes   sunlight
> building   sustainable   electricity   heat

Solar energy was used in the new building. [1] .... shines into these tubes. It's reflected through the tubes by a [2] .... and it lights up the room. A special cover on top of each tube keeps the [3] .... outside. Then large [4] ....were made and the [5] .... were placed inside them. For even more [6] .... energy [7] .... were built. When the panels receive sunlight, they turn it into [8] .... Solar panels can create enough energy to power the whole [9] .....

7 ▶ **8.2** Watch the video again and check your answers to Exercises 5 and 6.

Your turn

8 Discuss the questions in groups.

1 What are the most common natural disasters in your country?
2 Are there any buildings in your town with solar panels?
3 Do many people have solar panels on their houses in your town?
4 Do you think solar panels are a good idea? Why/ Why not?

In my country, we have terrible forest fires ...

Reading An article

1 **Work with a partner. Look at the photos and answer the questions.**

1 What can you see in each photo?

2 What connects the photos?

2 🔊 **2.42** **Read the article about renewable energy. Match the renewable energies in the photos with the countries in the text.**

3 **Read the article again and answer the questions.**

1 Where does Minnesota get its biomass from?

2 What two benefits does using biomass have for the environment?

3 Why is the sun so important in Australia?

4 What two results has the use of solar power had in Australia?

5 Why has Britain got lots of sea and wind?

6 Which wind farm will produce more electricity?

Explore phrasal verbs

4 **Look at the highlighted words in the text. Match the phrasal verbs (1–5) with the definitions (a–e).**

1	bring down	a	build
2	keep on	b	cut so it falls to the ground
3	put up	c	reduce/make smaller
4	knock down	d	fall to the ground
5	cut down	e	continue

➡ **Vocabulary Bank • page 114**

Your turn

5 **Make notes about the questions.**

1 Why is renewable energy important for our world?

2 What renewable energy is used in your country?

3 What do you do to save energy at home or at school?

6 **Ask and answer the questions in Exercise 5 with your partner. Use your notes to help you.**

THREE **COUNTRIES,** THREE **RENEWABLES**

Humans are capable of producing energy that – unlike oil, natural gas and coal – do not damage the environment. We look at three countries and three different renewable energy sources.

The USA

The USA has several renewable energy projects. A lot of power stations use biomass to produce energy. Biomass is anything natural – plants and trees mostly – and it can be used to produce electricity. In a recent storm in Minnesota, over 3,000 trees were **knocked down** by strong winds. The wood from the trees was burned to produce energy. The state also wants to **cut down** 40,000 more trees because they are diseased. Of course, new trees are planted in place of the old ones, which also helps the environment.

USA

Australia

It's certainly sunny in Australia. The country gets more than 3,500 hours of sunlight a year – that's ten hours a day – and solar energy is big business. Australia has spent a lot of money on solar energy. Solar panels power houses, schools, businesses and factories all over the country. About a quarter of all homes in South Australia use solar power. Australian solar power has **brought down** the country's energy bills and has had a very positive environmental effect. If Australia **keeps on** spending money on energy, it is thought that by 2030, 100% of Australia's energy could come from renewable sources.

Australia

The UK

Everyone knows that in the UK it's not sunny very often! Britain only gets between 1,200 and 1,600 hours of sunlight a year. So it's clear that solar power isn't big in Britain. But Britain has other renewable sources that can produce energy. It's an island so the British government is taking advantage of the often windy conditions and is **putting up** wind farms off its coasts. In Cumbria, in the north-west of England, enough energy is produced by more than 100 turbines to power over 320,000 homes. On the other side of the country, there is a wind farm with 88 wind turbines off the coast of Norfolk.

wind turbines

biomass

solar panels

FACT! *The Earth gets enough sunlight in one hour to give energy to the whole world for one year.*

91

Speaking Apologising and explaining

Real talk: Do you do any volunteer work?

1 ▶ **8.3** **Watch the teenagers in the video. Which volunteer work do they do?**

- babysitting
- help in after-school clubs
- cleaning the school
- read to older people
- pick up litter
- teach children English
- help in school garden
- help older people with their animals

2 💬 **Do *you* do any volunteer work?**

3 🔊 **2.43** **Jessica meets her friend Oliver. How many excuses does Jessica give?**

4 **Complete the conversation with the useful language.**

Useful language

I'm really sorry.
I'm sorry.
I really meant to come, honest!
I completely forgot.

Oh well, never mind.
The thing is, …
I'll (come next week), I promise.
The problem was, …

Oliver:	Hello Jessica. What happened to you **yesterday**?
Jessica:	**Yesterday**? What do you mean?
Oliver:	We were **planting vegetables in the school garden**.
Jessica:	Oh, yes! I'm ¹..*sorry*... I completely ²…. .
Oliver:	Jessica, I **sent you a text** to remind you!
Jessica:	Yes, I know, I really ³…. to come, honest! The problem ⁴…. **my alarm clock was broken**.
Oliver:	Well it was only **a couple of hours**, not **all day**.
Jessica:	Yes, I know. I ⁵…. sorry, Oliver. ⁶…. is, I **had a lot of chores to do too** and because I **slept late, I didn't have time**.
Oliver:	Oh well, ⁷…. mind. How about **next week**? We're planning to **plant some fruit trees**.
Jessica:	Great! I'll come **next week**, ⁸…. !

5 🔊 **2.43** **Listen again and check your answers.**

6 💬 **Work with a partner. Practise the conversation in Exercise 4.**

7 💬 **Change the words in bold in the conversation. Use the information below. Take turns to apologise to a friend and explain what the problem was.**

Situation 1

You forgot to go with your friend to see an exhibition about Earthships. Now your friend is angry.

Situation 2

You didn't help your friend write an article about recycling. Now your friend is angry.

✎ Writing A newspaper article

1 **Look at the photos and read the article from a school newspaper. What did the volunteers do?**

A RIVER OF HELP

LAST SUNDAY ABOUT 100 PEOPLE WENT TO LONGLEY NATURE RESERVE TO CLEAN UP THE RIVER. *THE EVENT* WAS ORGANISED BY THE CLEANUPRIVERS PROJECT, WHICH HELPS TO PROTECT THE ENVIRONMENT.

'Every summer local volunteers collect rubbish which is thrown in the river,' John Sanders, from Cleanuprivers told me. This time I was one of them. We picked up hundreds of plastic bottles, food packets and drinks cans. But that's not all that's in the river. 'We also found car tyres, a fridge and an old bed!' one volunteer said.

The clean-up also removes non-native plants from the river. These plants kill off native species and affect biodiversity. At Longley we cut down Himalayan Balsam. 'It's a beautiful plant, but dangerous because it covers everything,' said the local plant expert, Lynn Douglas. The clean-up was hard work but fun, and the river looked great! So when is the next event? Check the Cleanuprivers.org web page.   Report by Chris Davies

2 **Read the newspaper article again. Put the information in the correct order.**

- What is happening next?
- When did they do it? *1*
- What did they do?
- What was the opinion of the event?
- Who was involved?

Useful language

Using direct speech
When writing newspaper articles, use direct quotes.
'Every summer, … in the river,' John Sanders … told me.

3 **Look at the Useful language box. Find more examples of direct speech in the text. What is the punctuation for exclamations?**

4 **Write these direct speech sentences with the correct punctuation.**

1 What happened to the river she asked
   'What happened to the river?' she asked.
2 It's amazing said Abby
3 Meet me at the river she told me
4 We have to clear out all this rubbish she said
5 Are you coming to the next event I asked Tom

✎ Get writing

PLAN

5 **Plan your newspaper article about an event (sport, cultural) in your area. Make notes on the things in Exercise 2 and use the same structure.**

WRITE

6 **Write your essay. Use your notes from Exercise 5 and the model text to help you.**

CHECK

7 **Can you say YES to these questions?**

- Is the information from the plan in your article?
- Have you used some direct speech in your article?

7–8 Review

Vocabulary

1 Complete the text with the correct form of the words in the box.

> bullying   hand in homework   get detention
> cheat in a test   on time   ~~wear a uniform~~
> get good marks   write lines

I like my school but there are a few rules that we have to follow. We have to ¹ *wear a uniform* – it's a white shirt and a black skirt or trousers. In the morning, if you aren't ² ...., you have to write your name in the late book. We have to ³ .... on Friday morning – we get it twice a week. If we forget we ⁴ .... – this means we have to stay after school and ⁵ ..... I study hard and I usually ⁶ ..... I've never ⁷ .... and anyone who tries to cheat gets into trouble. All the students in my school are kind and friendly – there's no ⁸ .... – it's a great school.

2 Complete the phrases with *make* or *do*.

1 *make* a mistake
2 .... something interesting
3 .... friends
4 .... your homework
5 .... a phone call
6 .... the right thing

3 Write the material for each object.

1 *glass*

4 Complete the text with the words in the box.

> ~~consume~~   saves   leave   wastes
> reduce   switch off   turn down

People generally ¹ *consume* a large amount of energy every day. There are a number of ways to ² .... your energy bills and help the environment at the same time. ³ .... your heating in the winter – wear an extra sweater instead! Using cold water to wash clothes also ⁴ .... energy. ⁵ .... appliances when you are not using them. Some people ⁶ .... their TV or computer on standby all night and that ⁷ .... a lot of electricity.

Explore vocabulary

5 Complete the text with the words in the box.

> ~~propose~~   vote   together   throw away
> shaped   match   decorations   reuse (x2)

Adam:	We need to decide on the theme for the end-of-school party. What does everyone ¹ *propose* ?
Bella:	What about a ball with an eco theme?
Adam:	Okay. What do you mean?
Bella:	Well, we could ² .... coloured waste paper to make ³ .... .
Chris:	That's a good idea – we ⁴ .... a lot of paper and it's a good way to ⁵ .... it.
Adam:	Good, so who wants to make them?
Chris:	Bella and I can do that ⁶ .... .
Bella:	Could we have paper plates ⁷ .... like leaves?
Chris:	How does that ⁸ .... the eco theme?
Bella:	Trees – the environment ...
Adam:	Oh okay, yes. Right, let's ⁹ .... . Who's in favour of the eco-theme ball?
All:	Yes!

6 Complete the text with the words in the box.

> ~~pick up~~   find out   write out   work out
> try out   keep on   put up   knock down
> cut down

1 George *picked up* French really quickly when we went to Paris.
2 My dad .... a tree house for us in our garden when we were young.
3 I'm going to .... my new bike at the weekend.
4 **A:** I can't .... the answer to this Maths problem.
   B: I know it's difficult, but you should .... trying to find the answer.
5 We need to .... about renewable energy in our country for a school project.
6 They had to .... that beautiful old tree in our street – it was dangerous.
7 Can you .... your full name and address here, please?
8 Did you know that they are going to .... that building? It's old and dangerous.

Language focus

1 Complete the sentences with the verbs in brackets. Use the second conditional.

1 If you _were_ (be) more confident, you _would make_ (make) make more friends.
2 If he .... (not go) to school, he .... (be) bored.
3 If they .... (wear) uniforms, they .... (look) the same.
4 We .... (have) more free time if we .... (not have) so much homework.
5 You .... (not be) so tired if you .... (not stay) up late.
6 If she .... (study) harder, she .... (get) better marks at school.

2 Write questions using the second conditional.

1 What / you / do / if / you / see someone cheating in a test?
   What would you do if you saw someone cheating in a test?
2 Where / you / live / if / you / can go anywhere in the world?
3 If / you / win / 5,000 euros / what / you / do?
4 If / your friend / not answer / your email / what / you / say?
5 If / you / not pass / your next test / you / feel upset?

3 Write sentences using the present simple passive.

1 They recycle these metal tins. *These metal tins are recycled.*
2 They make these sweaters from plastic bottles.
3 They use corn to make heating oil.
4 They produce electricity from this water.
5 They build these houses from organic materials.
6 Solar energy heats the water.

4 Complete the sentences with the past passive of the verbs in the box. Then write a question for each statement.

discover	build	~~make~~	destroy	grow	not eat

1 The first talking film _was made_ in 1927.
   When _was the first talking film made_ ?
2 Tea .... in China 4,000 years ago.
   When .... in China?
3 Gold .... in California in the 19th century.
   Where .... in the 19th century?
4 Pompeii .... by a volcanic eruption in 79AD.
   When .... by a volcanic eruption?
5 Tomatoes .... in Europe until the 16th century.
   When .... in Europe?
6 The first public railways .... in England in the 19th century.
   Where .... ?

Language builder

5 Choose the correct words to complete the conversation.

Tom: If you [1] _a_ your own blog on the Internet, what [2] .... about?

Hanna: About the environment. Lots of blogs about the environment [3] .... on the Internet, but not many of them [4] .... for teenagers. I want to help the planet. If we [5] .... something now, then it [6] .... too late.

Tom: I agree. I read about a music blog. It [7] .... by a teenager a couple of years ago. It [8] .... by thousands of people and later he became a music journalist.

Hanna: So if my blog [9] .... popular, then someone [10] .... me a job as a journalist, too!

Tom: Who knows? I think I [11] .... a blog. Let's write it together.

	a	b	c
1	wrote	would write	will write
2	will it be	would it be	is it
3	published	are published	publish
4	are written	are writing	are write
5	are not doing	not do	don't do
6	is	would be	will be
7	started	was starting	was started
8	read	was reading	was read
9	becomes	is becoming	would become
10	will probably give	gives probably	probably is giving
11	started	might start	am starting

Speaking

6 Match the sentences.

1 I need your advice.   *b*
2 What do you think I should do?
3 I'm really sorry.
4 I sent you a text to remind you!
5 Have you tried talking to him?
6 Oh well, how about next week?

a If I were you, I wouldn't listen to him.
b What's the problem?
c Yes, I know. I really meant to come, honest!
d No, I haven't – that's a good idea.
e Okay, never mind.
f Yes, great, I'll come.

Say it right!

Unit 1 /ɪ/ and /iː/

1 🔊 **1.06** **Listen and repeat.**
/ɪ/ wind   city   /iː/ freeze   beach

2 🔊 **1.07** **Listen and choose.**

	/i/	/ɪː/
1	it	eat
2	live	leave
3	hit	heat
4	ship	sheep
5	fill	feel

3 **Match the words to the correct sound.**

> ~~extreme~~ free heat ~~give~~ listen
> six swim teach

/ɪ/ *give*   /iː/ *extreme*

4 🔊 **1.08** **Listen, check and repeat.**

Unit 2 Word stress

1 🔊 **1.22** **Listen and repeat.**

> orchestra invention microphone tomorrow
> Internet computer important instrument

2 🔊 **1.23** **Listen again and match the words to the correct stress pattern.**

ȯrchestra	invėntion

3 🔊 **1.23** **Listen, check and repeat.**

4 **Add the words to the chart.**

> develop concentrate exercise creative
> Saturday correctly

5 🔊 **1.24** **Listen, check and repeat.**

Unit 3 Strong and weak forms of *have*

1 🔊 **1.35** **Listen and repeat.**
1 **Have** you ever been to Rome?
2 Yes, I **have**.
3 I**'ve** seen the film, but I **haven't** read the book.

2 🔊 **1.36** **Listen to the conversations. Are the forms of *have* strong or weak?**
1 A: [1]**Have** you ever eaten shark?
   B: Shark? No, I [2]**haven't**.
   A: Well, [3]I**'ve** tried it and it's delicious. What about jellyfish? [4]**Have** you tried that?
   B: Yes, I [5]**have**.
   A: I [6]**haven't** tried it, but it sounds horrible!
2 A: [1]I**'ve** just finished reading *The Hunger Games*. [2]**Have** you ever read it?
   B: No, I [3]**haven't**. Are those books good?
   A: Yes! [4]**Have** you seen the films?
   B: Yes, I [5]**have**, but [6]I**'ve** only seen the first film.

3 🔊 **1.36** **Listen, check and repeat.**

4 **Work with a partner. Practise the conversations in Exercise 2.**

Unit 4 Consonant to vowel linking

1 🔊 **1.46** **Listen and repeat.**
1 The school day starts at eight o'clock.
2 We set off early in the morning.

2 🔊 **1.47** **Listen and mark the links between consonant and vowel sounds.**
1 We visited a big city. (1 link)
2 Did you find out what happened at the party? (2 links)
3 Let's look around the town after lunch. (2 links)
4 Chill out! The exam isn't until Friday. (3 links)
5 How do you chill out? (1 link)
6 What languages are easy to pick up? (2 links)

3 🔊 **1.47** **Listen, check and repeat.**

Say it right!

Unit 5 Intonation in first conditional sentences

1 🔊 `2.08` **Listen and repeat.**

1 If you speak good English, you'll get a better job.

2 I'll go to university if I pass my exams.

2 🔊 `2.09` **Listen and mark the fall-rising (⤩) and falling (⬎) intonation on the stressed words in the sentences.**

1 If he doesn't call, I'll send him a message.
2 You'll meet my friends if you get there early.
3 If you don't listen to me, you won't understand.
4 I'll make more friends in London if I speak good English.
5 He'll help if we have a problem.
6 If we get homework, I won't go out.

3 🔊 `2.09` **Listen, check and repeat.**

4 **Practise saying the sentences in Exercise 2 with the correct intonation.**

Unit 6 *ough*

1 🔊 `2.19` **Listen and repeat.**

> enough   through   thought   although

2 🔊 `2.20` **Listen and choose the correct sound.**

1 I think that's en**ough**.   /ʌ/   /uː/
2 We walked thr**ough** the park.   /ʌ/   /uː/
3 I th**ough**t it was scary.   /ɔː/   /uː/
4 Alth**ough** I like her, she's not my best friend.   /ʌ/   /əʊ/
5 I b**ough**t a new T-shirt yesterday. /ɔː/   /uː/
6 Even th**ough** I'm afraid of insects, I like butterflies.   /ʌ/   /əʊ/

3 🔊 `2.20` **Listen, check and repeat.**

Unit 7 Intonation in second conditional sentences

1 🔊 `2.26` **Listen and repeat.**

1 If I was rude to the teacher, I'd get detention.

2 I'd study Art if I went to a Free school.

2 🔊 `2.27` **Listen and mark the fall-rising (⤩) and falling (⬎) intonation on the stressed words in the sentences.**

1 If I was headteacher of my school, I would make the lunch breaks longer.
2 If you lived in the UK, your life would be different.
3 I wouldn't give any homework if I was a teacher.
4 I'd go to the cinema if it was my birthday tomorrow.

3 🔊 `2.27` **Listen, check and repeat.**

4 **Practise saying the sentences in Exercise 2 with the correct intonation.**

Unit 8 Stress in compound words

1 🔊 `2.35` **Listen and repeat.**

> metal **cans**   glass **bottle**   **car** tyre
> **earth**quake   cotton **T-shirt**   solar **energy**

2 **Mark the stress on the compound words.**

> birthday cake   sun cream   leather shoes
> paper plates   sun hat   sweet wrappers
> plastic glasses   brick wall
> swimming pool   plastic table

3 🔊 `2.36` **Listen, check and repeat.**

Grammar reference

Starter Unit

Wh- questions

- We usually make questions by changing the word order. We put the auxiliary verb before the subject.
  Where do you live?
- In present simple questions we use *do/does*.
  What time does the film start?
- In past simple questions we use *did*.
  How did you do in your exam?
- We don't use *do/does/did* in questions when *who/what/which* is the subject of the sentence.
  Who texted Ben? (subject)
  Who did Ben text? (object)

Comparatives and superlatives

	Comparative	Superlative
1 or 2 syllable	adjective + -*er* / -*ier*	(*the*) adjective + -*est* / -*iest*
Adjectives	old – old**er**	old – the old**est**
	happy – happ**ier**	happy – the happ**iest**
3 or more syllables	more + adjective **more** interesting	(the) most + adjective **the most** interesting
Irregular forms	good – **better**	good – **the best**
good* and *bad	bad – **worse**	bad – **the worst**

- We use comparative and superlative forms to compare things. To make comparative forms we add -*er* to 1 and 2 syllable adjectives. When the adjective ends in -*y*, we change it to an -*i*.
  My dad's tall but my uncle is taller.
  Kelly's friendly but Sam's friendlier.

Adjectives and adverbs

quiet	quietly	bad	badly
happy	happily	easy	easily
sad	sadly	quick	quickly
good	well	careful	carefully

- Adjectives tell us about a noun. We use adjectives before nouns and after some verbs, especially *be*.
  Alice is a good student.
  Please be quiet.
- Adverbs tell us about verbs. An adverb tells us how somebody does something or how something happens.
  Jack painted the picture carefully.
  Please speak quietly.

Comparative and superlative adverbs

- In general, comparative and superlative forms of adverbs are the same as for adjectives. With adverbs ending in -*ly*, we use *more* for the comparative and *most* for the superlative:

Adverb	Comparative	Superlative
quie**tly**	**more** quietly	**most** quietly
slow**ly**	**more** slowly	**most** slowly
serious**ly**	**more** seriously	**most** seriously

Could you talk more quietly? ~~Could you talk quietlier?~~
The teacher spoke more slowly.

- Some adverbs have irregular comparative forms.

Adverb	Comparative	Superlative
badly	worse	worst
far	farther/further	farthest/furthest
little	less	least
well	better	best

You're driving worse today than yesterday.
The girl ran further than the boy.

Past simple

- We use the past simple to talk about completed events and actions in the past. We form regular past tense forms by adding -*ed*.
  I played football yesterday.
  I walked to school this morning.
- We form the negative of the past simple with subject + *didn't* + infinitive.
  I didn't go the cinema.
- We form past simple questions with *did* + subject + infinitive.
  Did she enjoy the party? Yes, she did.
- We form *Wh-* question in the past simple with Question word + *did* + subject + infinitive.
  What did you do on holiday?
- Some verbs are irregular in the past simple. They don't follow any pattern. (See irregular verbs list on page 126.)
- *Was* and *were* are the past simple forms of *be*.
  He was in town for two hours.
- To form *Yes/No* questions, we use *was/were* before the subject. We don't use *do*.
  Was he happy? Were the cats eating?
- To form *Wh-* questions, we put the question word before *was/were*.
  What film was it?
  When were you at the park?

Grammar reference

Unit 1

Present simple vs. present continuous

- We use the present simple to talk about facts, habits and routines.
  My sister likes cold weather.
  I go to school early every day.
  He doesn't like fish.
  We don't live in Malaga.
  Do you live in France?
  Where does she live?
- We use the present continuous to talk about actions in progress at the time of speaking or around that time.
  Silvia is driving to work this week.
  I'm working on my school project at the moment.
- We form the affirmative with subject + *be* + verb + *-ing*.
  I'm reading.
  They're listening.
- We form the negative with *be not* + verb + *-ing*. *Not* is usually contracted.
  You aren't listening.
  She isn't sleeping.
- We form questions, with *be* + subject + verb + *-ing*.
  Is Ana doing her homework?
- In information questions, we put the *Wh-* question word before *be*.
  Where are they shopping?
  What book is he reading?

1 **Complete the conversation. Use the present simple or the present continuous form of the verbs in brackets.**

John:	Hello. ¹…. (you do) anything at the moment?
Katie:	Right now, I ²…. (look after) my brother. Why?
John:	What time ³…. (your mum get) home?
Katie:	She ⁴…. (work) late every Thursday, so at about half past seven. Why?
John:	They ⁵…. (show) that new comedy film at the cinema in town. It ⁶…. (start) at half past eight. My sister and I ⁷…. (think) about going. ⁸…. (you want) to come with us?
Katie:	Yes, please! Let's meet at the cinema at eight!

Adverbs of frequency

never   hardly ever   sometimes   usually   often   always

- We use adverbs of frequency to say how often something happens.
- We put them before the main verb but after the verb to *be*.
  It hardly ever snows here.
  There are often snowstorms here in winter.
- *Often*, *sometimes* and *usually* can also come at the beginning of the sentence.
  Sometimes, my family and I have barbecues.
- We use adverbs of frequency (*always, often, hardly ever* …) with the present simple. We use *at the moment* and *now* with the present continuous.
  My dad often plays computer games with me.
  My mum is running at the moment.

2 **Put the words in the correct order to make sentences.**

1. washes / the / Theo / never / car *Theo never washes the car.*
2. hardly / watch / TV / They / ever
3. late / sometimes / am / school / for / I
4. get / marks / exams / good / You / always / in
5. on / play / usually / We / football / Wednesdays
6. homework / with / often / She / helps me / my

Past simple vs. past continuous

* See Starter Unit for past simple.
- We use the past continuous to talk about actions in progress at a certain time in the past.
  At lunchtime, it was raining.
- We form affirmative sentences with subject + *was/were* + verb + *-ing*.
  He was crying.
  We weren't listening.
- We form the negative with *was/were* + *not* (*n't*) + verb + *-ing*. *Not* is usually contracted.
  They weren't helping to tidy.

3 **Complete the text. Use the past simple or the past continuous form of the verbs in brackets.**
When I woke up, it ¹ *was raining* (rain). I ²…. (walk) to the bathroom, but my brother ³…. (have) a shower. I ⁴…. (tell) him to be quick and then I ⁵…. (go) to the kitchen. Dad ⁶…. (read) the newspaper, and Mum ⁷…. (listen) to the news.' ⁸…. (you sleep) well?' asked Dad. 'No,' I said, 'I ⁹…. (have) a very strange dream about a horse in my English class!

Grammar reference

Unit 2

should

+	I/You/He/She/It/We/You/They	should	help.
-	I/You/He/She/It/We/You/They	shouldn't	
?	Should		help?
+	Yes,	I/you/he/she/it/we/you/they	should.
+	No,		shouldn't.

- We use *should* to say what we think is a good idea, or important to do.
  You should organise a party for your birthday.
  They should ask the teacher.
- *Should* is the same in all forms.
- We use an infinitive without *to* after *should*.
  John should ~~to~~ get more sleep.

1 Complete the questions and sentences with the correct form of *should* and the verbs in the box.

> invite   ~~try~~   not play   listen   wear   not talk

1 You ..*should try*.. harder – you can do it!
2 She .... her music loudly.
3 What .... I .... to the party?
4 They .... in here – it's a library.
5 .... we .... Leo to the cinema with us?
6 He .... to the teacher in class.

must

+	I/You/He/She/It/We/You/They	must	go.
-		mustn't	
?	Must		go?
+	Yes,	I/you/he/she/it/we/you/they	must.
-	No,		mustn't.

- We use *must* to say what we think is necessary to do.
  You must listen to this song. It's fantastic!
- We use *mustn't* to say what we think is necessary not to do.
  We mustn't forget to buy her a present.
- *Must* is the same in all forms.
- We use the infinitive without *to* after *must*.
  You must remember that story. (~~You must to remember that story.~~)

2 Choose the correct words.

1 You **should** / (**mustn't**) forget to call me tonight.
2 Students **should** / **mustn't** run in the corridors.
3 You **must** / **shouldn't** stay up so late – you're tired today.
4 I think they **must** / **should** relax more.
5 We **shouldn't** / **mustn't** be noisy in the library.

have to/don't have to

+	I/We/You/They	have to	practise.
	He/She/It	has to	
-	I/We/You/They	don't have to	
	He/She/It	doesn't have to	
?	Do	I/we/you/they	have to practise.
	Does	he/she/it	
+	Yes,	I/we/you/they	do.
		he/she/it	does.
-	No,	I/we/you/they	don't.
		he/she/it	doesn't.

- We use *have to* to say what is necessary to do.
  You have to answer all the questions in the exam.
  Toby has to look after his sister this afternoon.
- We use *don't have to* to say what isn't necessary to do, but is an option or a choice.
  I don't have to help you with the homework.
  Elsie doesn't have to get up early tomorrow.
- Question words go at the beginning of the question.
  How much homework do you have to do?
  When do we have to make a decision?

3 Complete the sentences and questions with the correct form of *have to*.

1 You *don't have to* phone. You can email for information.
2 At my school, we .... play hockey, but there is a school team.
3 Doctors .... study for seven or eight years.
4 Why .... she .... do the exam again?
5 .... we .... bring our instruments with us?

4 Complete the sentences with *don't have to*, *doesn't have to* or *mustn't*.

1 He *doesn't have to* get up early tomorrow.
2 He .... eat in here – it isn't allowed.
3 I .... give this to the teacher until Friday.
4 She .... use those scissors – they're dangerous.
5 You .... forget to feed the cat.

Grammar reference

Unit 3

Present perfect for indefinite past time

+	I/We/You/They	have passed	the exam.	
+	He/She/It	has passed		
-	I/We/You/They	haven't passed		
-	He/She/It	hasn't passed		
?	Have	I/we/you/they	passed	the exam?
?	Has	he/she/it		
+	Yes,	I/we/you/they	have.	
+		he/she/it	has.	
-	No,	I/we/you/they	haven't.	
-		he/she/it	hasn't.	

- We use the present perfect to talk about experiences and facts in the past when the exact time is not mentioned or important.
  The school have organised a trip to Germany.
  I've seen some fantastic graffiti.
- We form the affirmative with subject + *have/has* + past participle.
  I've bought tickets for the exhibition.
  She's given me some good advice.
- We form the negative with subject + *haven't/hasn't* + past participle.
  Max hasn't seen the mural.
  They haven't asked me for help.
- Regular past participles end in *-ed, -d* or *-ied.*
  want–wanted   believe–believed
  play–played   worry–worried
- Many common verbs have irregular past participles.
  go–gone   put–put
  see–seen   hear–heard
- We use *be (been)* to say somebody has returned from a place or from doing an activity.
- We use *go (gone)* to say somebody has not returned from a place or from doing an activity.
  He's gone shopping. (He is at the shop now.)
  He's been shopping. (He has returned.)

1 Complete the sentences. Use the present perfect form of the verbs in brackets.

1 *I've finished* washing the car. (finish)
2 We .... so many great paintings today. (see)
3 Your postcard from Tom ..... . (not arrive)
4 You .... a letter to your aunty. (not write)
5 They .... visiting the museums. (enjoy)
6 She .... to Leo four times this week. (speak)

Present perfect with *ever/never*

?	Have	I/we/you/they	ever	seen	the film?
?	Has	he/she/it			
+	I/We/You/They	have	never		the film.
+	He/She/It	has			

- We often use *ever* in present perfect questions when the exact time isn't important.
  Has she ever had piano lessons?
  Have you every broken your arm or leg?
- We often use *never* to say not at any time when answering these questions.
  He's never met anybody famous.
  I've never lived in another city. I've only ever lived here.

2 Look at the table. Write present perfect questions with *ever*. Then write the correct answers.

	Charlotte	Aiden and Milo	You
climb a mountain	1 ✓	5 ✗	9 ?
win a prize	2 ✗	6 ✓	10 ?
go to a music festival	3 ✗	7 ✓	11 ?
make a cake	4 ✓	8 ✗	12 ?

1 *Has Charlotte ever climbed a mountain? Yes, she has.*

3 Complete the conversation. Use the present perfect form of the verbs in brackets.

A: ¹ .....*Have*..... you .....*heard*..... (hear) the new Kaiser Chiefs CD?
B: No, I ² .... I prefer pop music.
A: Oh! What bands ³ .... you .... (see) in concert?
B: I ⁴ .... (never see) a band in concert. I don't like loud noise and lots of people.
A: I love it! I ⁵ .... (be) to lots of concerts. ⁶ .... you .... (ever be) to the small concerts in town?
B: No, I ⁷ .... .
A: I ⁸ .... (buy) two tickets to see a new band this weekend. Do you want to come?
B: Maybe. I ⁹ .... (not finish) my homework and my mum ¹⁰ .... (ask) me to help her too.
A: Come on!
B: OK!

Grammar reference

Unit 4

Present perfect with *still, yet, already* and *just*

- We often use *still, yet, already* and *just* with the present perfect.
  Jack's already been to Australia three times.
  I haven't had time to go shopping yet.
  We still haven't decided where to go on holiday.
  Dad's just got home and he's feeling tired.
- We use *still* with negative verbs to express that something we expected has not happened, but imagine it will happen in the future. We put *still* directly after the subject.
  My uncle still hasn't telephoned.
- We use *yet* with negative verbs to emphasise that something we expected has not happened. We put *yet* after the complete verb phrase.
  John hasn't arrived yet.
- We use *yet* in questions to ask about things we don't think have happened.
  Have you bought the train tickets yet?
- We use *already* to explain that something happened before we expected or to emphasise it has happened. We usually put *already* between *have* and the past participle.
- We use *just* with the present perfect to talk about very recent events and actions.
  I've just heard the good news. It's fantastic!

1 Complete the sentences with *still, yet, already* or *just*.

1 You ....*still*.... haven't bought me a birthday present.
2 I haven't seen the *Superman* film .... .
3 Harry's .... broken his new computer.
4 They haven't asked their parents .... .
5 I've .... had some juice.
6 Lucy .... hasn't decided what she wants to do at university.

2 Complete the sentences. Use the present perfect with *still, yet, already* or *just* and the phrases in the box.

> not eat   ~~have some juice~~   start   see   not hear

1 Do you want a drink?
  No, thanks. I've *just had some juice* .
2 What do you think of the news?
  I don't know. I .... .
3 Do you want to watch this DVD?
  Not really. I .... it.
4 Do the children want some sweets?
  No, they .... their dinner .... .
5 Sorry, I'm late.
  It's OK. We .... .

Present perfect with *for* and *since*

- We use *for* and *since* with the present perfect to say how long something has been true.
  I've lived here since I was seven.
  She hasn't gone climbing for three years.
- We use *for* with periods of time.
  My parents have been married for twenty-one years.
- We use *since* with a reference to a specific time.
  I've known her since 2009.
  Emma and Anna haven't spoken since the party.

3 Complete the table with the words in the box.

> ~~three weeks~~   Monday   2008   a long time
> two hours   last December   this morning
> months   twelve weeks

for	since
three weeks	

Present perfect vs. past simple

- We use the past simple when the moment in which something happened has ended. When it happened isn't always mentioned, usually because it is clear.
  I went to Liverpool in June. (It's now July.)
- We use the present perfect when something started or happened in the past and continues to be true. We can say how long something has been true, but not when it started.
  I've been to Liverpool. (When isn't specified, but continues to be true.)
  They've begun the exam. (The exam hasn't finished.)

4 Complete the conversation. Use the present perfect or the past simple form of the verbs in brackets.

> **Mum:** Sam, [1] ....*Have you seen*.... (you/see) Julia?
> **Sam:** No, I [2] .... (not see) her since last night. We [3] .... (watch) TV but she was tired, so she [4] .... (go) to bed. Why?
> **Mum:** She isn't here and she [5] .... (go) to school. Her teacher [6] .... (just call).
> **Sam:** I don't know. [7] .... (you ask) Dad?
> **Mum:** I rang the office, but he [8] .... (still not reply) to my message.
> **Julia:** Hi!
> **Mum:** Julia! Where [9] .... (you be)?
> **Julia:** Sorry, Mum. I [10] .... (not feel) very well, so I [11] .... (go) to the doctor.

Grammar reference

Unit 5

will, might/may

+	I/He/She/It/We/You/They	might/may	help.
-		might not/may not	
?	Might/May	I/he/she/it/we/you/they	help?
+	Yes,	I/he/she/it/we/you/they	might/may.
-	No,		might not/may not.

- We can use *will* and *might/may* to give our opinions about the future.
  When she gets here, she'll want to speak to you.
  I might travel round the world next year.
  She may go to India next year.
- We use *will* and *won't* to show we are sure about the future.
  We'll go to the party later.
  She won't text you because she's angry with you.
- We use *might/may* and *might not/may not* to show we are not sure about the future.
  I might go to the party later. (I'm not sure.)
  She may not call you if she's busy.
- We use an infinitive without *to* after *will* and *might/may*.
  He'll to go shopping.   He may to go out later.

1 Complete the conversations with *might (not)/may (not)* or *will* and the ideas in brackets.

1 A: What are you doing this weekend?
  B: I'm not sure. I ...*might stay in*... . (stay in)
2 A: Where are you going to meet Megan?
  B: We haven't decided. We ..... (at the park)
3 A: I hope she gets the tickets.
  B: Relax. The stadium is really big – the tickets ..... (not sell out)
4 A: I've bought Harry a birthday present.
  B: I'm sure he ..... (love it)
5 A: When is Paula going to see Ethan?
  B: I think ..... (on Thursday)

Adverbs of possibility

- We often use adverbs after *will* and *might* to emphasise our feelings about the future.
- We often use *definitely* and *certainly* with *will* to emphasise we are sure about a future event or action.
  I'll definitely have a look at the website this evening.
  They certainly won't win the match against Liverpool.
- We often use *probably* with *will* to emphasise we are not completely sure about a future action or event.
  Natalie will probably be interested in this.

2 Choose the correct words.

1 I'll (probably) / certainly buy the red one, but I'm going to think about it.
2 She'll **definitely / probably** be late. She always is!
3 We **definitely will / 'll definitely** do it.
4 They **will probably / certainly will** need some help.
5 He **probably / definitely** won't know, but ask!
6 Computers **will certainly / definitely will** take over the world – the question is when!

First conditional + *may/might, be able to*

	Situation	Consequence
+	If I pass all my exams,	my parents might buy me a present.
-	If I don't pass all my exams,	my parents won't buy me a present.
	Consequence	**Situation**
-	My parents may not buy me a present	if I don't pass all my exams.
?	Will my parents buy me a present	if I pass all my exams?

- We use the first conditional to talk about possible situations in the present or future and say what we think the result will be.
- We often use *if* and the present simple to describe the possible action or event.
  If he doesn't email me, I won't speak to him again.
- We use *will/won't* + infinitive when we are sure of the result.
  If we don't leave now, we won't catch the 8.30 bus.
- We use *may/might (not)* to show we are less sure about the consequence.
  If she sees you, she might leave.
- We use *be able to* to talk about possible abilities.
  I'll be able to buy it if I save the money.
- When we use *if* to start the sentence, we use a comma between the two parts.
  If I see him, I'll give him the present.
  I'll give him the present if I see him

3 Complete the sentences with the correct form of the verb phrases in the box.

> not listen careful   speak quietly   not remind them
> tell him to call me   ~~go to the park~~

1 If it's sunny tomorrow, we'*ll go to the park* .
2 If you see him, ... you .... ?
3 You won't understand if you ..... .
4 They might not do it if you ..... .
5 He won't be frightened if you ..... .

Grammar reference

Unit 6

be going to/will/Present continuous

+	I	'm		tell him.
	He/She/It	's		
	We/You/They	're		
-	I	'm not	going to	
	He/She/It	isn't		
	We/You/They	aren't		
?	Am	I		tell him?
	Is	he/she/it		
	Are	we/you/they		

- We use *be going to* to talk about future actions we intend to do.
  After we finish school, I'm going to go to work.
  My grandparents are going to stay with us at the weekend.
- We use *will* to talk about predictions in the future.
  She won't find it – she always gets lost!
  They'll be late for the party. They always are.
  *See unit 5 for how we form *will*.
- We use the present continuous to talk about future arrangements when they have a fixed date.
  They're getting married this summer.
  She isn't coming to the party.
  *See unit 1 for how we form the present continuous.

1 Choose the correct form to complete the conversation.

> **A:** What time ¹(are you catching)/ will you catch the bus to London?
>
> **B:** Eleven o'clock – so I ² will leave / 'm leaving in ten minutes. I ³ will / 'm going to meet Alex at the bus station.
>
> **A:** What ⁴ are you going to / will you do in London?
>
> **B:** Well, I think the weather ⁵ will be / is being nice so we ⁶ will / 're going to take a boat ride along the Thames. Then we've got tickets for a walking tour so we're ⁷ going to meet / meeting our guide at one o'clock in Trafalgar Square.
>
> **A:** That sounds like fun. Have a great time.

Quantifiers – *how much/many, (not) enough, too many/much*

	Countable (plural)	uncountable	both
+	a few	a little	(not) enough
-	too many	too much	(not) enough
?	too many	too much	(not) enough

- We use quantifiers to express the quantity of something.
- When the noun is countable we always use the plural form.
  My sister has got too many toys.
- We use *too* + *much/many* to say that an amount is excessive. The difference between *too much* and *too many* is the same as the difference between *much* and *many*. *Too much* is used with singular (uncountable) nouns; *too many* is used with plurals.
  There are too many books for one person to carry.
  They eat too much fast food.
- We use *how much/how many* to ask about quantity.
  How much money have you got?
  How many books are there?
- We use *enough* to say a quantity is sufficient and *not enough* to say a quantity is insufficient.
  I didn't have enough time to answer all the questions.
  We've got enough players to make two teams.

a little/a few

- We use *a little* and *a few* to express small quantities.
  I've got a few emails that I need to reply to.
  There's a little chocolate ice cream.
- Use *a few* with plural countable nouns.
  I've got a few questions about phobias.
- We use *a little* with uncountable nouns.
  Can I have a little sugar?

2 Complete the sentences with the words in the box.

> ~~too much~~   a few   enough
> how many   a little   too many

1 I had ...*too much*... coffee and now I can't sleep.
2 You've got .... sweets – put some back.
3 I don't think we have .... money for cake.
4 .... students are there in your class?
5 There's only .... milk left – should I buy some?
6 I've got .... things to do today.

Grammar reference

Unit 7

Second conditional – affirmative and negative

Imaginary situation	Possible consequence
(*if* + past simple)	(*would* + infinitive)
If you woke up earlier,	you would arrive on time.
If she didn't talk in class,	she wouldn't get detention.

Consequence	Situation
(*would* + infinitive)	(*if* + past simple)
You would arrive on time	if you woke up earlier.
She wouldn't get detention	if she didn't talk in class.

(The table has + next to the first and third sub-sections and – next to the second and fourth.)

- We use second conditional sentences to talk about imaginary situations and the possible consequences. Both parts can be affirmative or negative.
  We'd be in Berlin now if we'd caught the early train.
  If he didn't go to work, he wouldn't be so tired.
- We use *if* + past simple (affirmative or negative) to describe the imaginary situation.
  If I didn't have a dog, I'd like to have a cat.
- We use *would* (*not*) + infinitive to express an imaginary result we are sure of. When *would* is affirmative, we usually contract it '*d*. The negative is usually *wouldn't*.
  If she didn't like you, she wouldn't send you texts.
  They'd get better grades if they studied.
- We can use *was* or *were* in the *if* part of the sentence with *I*, *he/she* and *it*.
  I'd be quiet and not say anything if I were/was you.
  If my sister wasn't/weren't at university, I'd still have to share a bedroom.
- When we use *if* to start the sentence, use a comma between the two parts.
  If I had more money, I'd buy a new mobile.

1 **Match the sentence halves.**

1 If he went to India, .*e*.
2 She would love to see you ....
3 There would be less pollution ....
4 If I was a teacher, ...
5 You wouldn't believe me ....
6 If he joined the football team, ...

a if people didn't use their cars every day.
b he'd make lots of friends.
c if you had time to come.
d if I told you.
e he'd visit Bombay.
f I wouldn't give any homework.

2 **Complete the second conditional sentences. Use the correct form of the verbs in brackets.**

1 If I ...*had*... (have) time, I'd *learn* (learn) to play the guitar.
2 She .... (not be) late for school if she .... (get up) earlier.
3 If they .... (know) the answer, they .... (tell) you.
4 Mr Jones .... (help) you if you .... (ask) him nicely.
5 If I .... (meet) Will Smith, I .... (ask) for his autograph.
6 Our English .... (get) better if we .... (move) to New York.

Second conditional – questions

Imaginary situation	Possible consequence
(*if* + past simple)	(*would* + infinitive)
If I helped you with your homework,	would you lend me your MP3 player?
Would your dad take us to the concert	if you asked him?

- We form questions using *if* + past simple, *would*(*n't*) + subject + verb.
  If I told you a secret, would you promise not to tell?
  If I didn't reply to your messages, wouldn't you get angry?
  Wouldn't life be better if we had a five-day weekend?

3 **Complete the questions with *would* and the correct form of the verbs in the box.**

> catch   go   say   can   ~~have~~   need

1 If you ...*had*... a dog, what ...*would*... you call it?
2 If you didn't feel ill, where .... you .... today?
3 What time .... we arrive if we .... the earlier train?
4 If you .... be a character from a film, who .... you be?
5 If he asked you to go out, ... you .... yes?
6 Who .... you ask if you .... to borrow some money?

4 **Write second conditional questions with the prompts.**

1 we / share a bedroom / how often / we / argue?
   If we shared a bedroom, how often would we argue?
2 they / like / it / I / stop / speaking to them?
3 What / his parents / say / they / know?
4 you / can / have a super power / what / it / be?
5 you / live in England / come home / often?
6 you / be / me / what / you / do?

Grammar reference

Unit 8

Present simple passive

+	This bottle	is made	of plastic
+	These toys	are made	
-	This bottle	isn't made	
-	These toys	aren't made	
?	Is	this bottle made	of plastic?
?	Are	these toys	

Yes, it is/they are.	No, it isn't/they aren't.

- We use the passive to describe a process. We are usually not interested in, or don't know, who does this process.
  English is spoken in most shops and restaurants.
  Credit cards aren't accepted with ID.
- To form the present simple passive we use *is/are* (*not*) + past participle.
  Coffee isn't grown in Europe.
  The streets are cleaned on Sundays.
  * See page 126 for a list of irregular past participles.
- We form questions with *is/are* + subject + past participle. We put *Wh-* question words before *is/are*.
  Is the main square decorated in the holidays?
  When are the exam results emailed to students?
  How many photos are uploaded a week?

1 Use a word from each box to complete the sentences. Use the present simple passive.

bananas spaghetti cakes	drink catch cook
tea fish chocolate	bake make grow

1 *Tea is drunk* in most countries.
2 .... from cocoa beans.
3 .... in an oven.
4 .... in rivers and at sea.
5 .... in Jamaica.
6 .... in boiling water.

2 Rewrite the sentences using the present simple passive.

1 They clean the windows every month.
  The windows are cleaned every month
2 They don't update their blog every day.
3 People take a lot of photos on mobile phones.
4 The hotel serves breakfast from 7–10 am.
5 Do they give students a certificate at the end of the year?
6 People ask a lot of questions in my class.

Past simple passive

+	The rubbish was	thrown away.
+	The old chairs were	
-	The rubbish wasn't	
-	The old chairs weren't	
?	Was the rubbish	thrown away?
?	Were the old chairs	

Yes, it was/they were.	No, it wasn't/they weren't.

- We use the past simple passive to describe processes in the past.
  Last year, a trip to Italy was organised at the end of term
  The competition winners were given books.
- To form the past simple passive we use *was/were* (*not*) + past participle.
  The first Disney film was made in 1937.
  Some of us weren't invited to the party.
- To form questions we use *was/were* + subject + past participle. We put *Wh-* question words before *was/were*.
  Were the instructions written in English?
  How much money was taken from her bag?
  In which country was the telephone invented?

Passive + *by*

- We use *by* with the passive to show who was responsible for the actions.
  A lot of houses were destroyed by the fire.
  Who was the song Tell me a lie *recorded by? I think it was (recorded by) One Direction.*

3 Complete the text with the past passive form of the verbs in brackets. Use *by* when necessary.

Modern text messages, or SMS, [1] *were invented* (invent) in 1992. Early messages [2] .... (not write) on a mobile phone, they could only be sent from a computer to a phone. In 1993, the first mobile-to-mobile SMS service [3] .... (introduce) in Sweden. It wasn't immediately popular, but by 2011, an average of 19.9 billion texts [4] .... (send) people every day. In the same year, SMS messages [5] .... (replace) chat apps, such as WhatsApp. They [6] .... (use) to send 19 billion texts a day. Experts think this number is going to double in the next two years.

Vocabulary Bank

 Jog your memory!

1 Cover the rest of the page. How many words to describe extreme weather and survival essentials can you remember?

Extreme weather (page 9)

boiling	heavy rain
freezing	high winds
hail	snowstorm
heatwave	thunder and lightning

1 Look at the words in the box. Write sentences about when you have experienced these weather conditions.

I went on holiday to Spain last year. It was boiling.

2 Work with a partner. Talk about your sentences. Where were you and what was the weather like?

Survival essentials (page 12)

sun cream	map	first aid kit
water bottle	sleeping bag	camera
sunglasses	penknife	glasses
compass	torch	contact lenses

1 Look at the words in the box. What do you pack when you go on holiday?

2 Add three more items that you usually pack to the list.

 Explore prepositional phrases (page 15)

a ship	the Internet	the planet
both directions	the island	

1 Look at the words in the box. Write the words in the correct column.

in	on
	a ship

2 Add these words to the correct column.

October	South Africa	the middle
television	total	Earth

hail – granizar

 Study tip

Keep a record of all your new words. You can write a translation or a definition in your vocabulary notebook or on cards.

Vocabulary Bank

 ## Jog your memory!

1 Cover the rest of the page. How many words to describe priorities and performing can you remember?

Priorities (page 19)

chat with	around the house
do	for yourself
do	enough sleep
get	friends online
hang out	something creative
have time	sports
help	with friends

1 Turn to page 19. Look at the words for two minutes.

2 Can you remember them all? Match the words in the box to make expressions.

Performing (page 22)

act	on stage
dancing	orchestra
instruments	play (the piano)
microphone	voice

1 Look at the words in the box. Which things do you need to have lessons for?

2 Which words are verbs and which words are nouns?

act – verb

 ## Explore verb + noun collocations (page 20)

catch a cold	have a snack
concentrate in your lessons	surf the Internet
get more sleep	watch TV

1 Look at the words in the box. Talk to your partner about when you do these activities or when they happen.

I always catch a cold in the winter.

2 Match the collocations from the text on page 20. Which collocation is a verb + adjective?

get out	relaxed
catch up	a good night's sleep
get	of bed
feel	on sleep

 ## Explore prepositions (page 25)

between	near	over
in front of	of	until

1 Look at the words in the box. Write true and false sentences for you using the prepositions.

My house is near a river.

2 Work with a partner. Say your sentences and guess which sentences are true and which are false.

catch a cold (verb + noun)

feel relaxed (verb + adjective)

 ## Study tip

Write collocations together and make a note of the form.

Vocabulary Bank

 Jog your memory!

1 Cover the rest of the page. How many words to describe art and instruments can you remember?

Art around us (page 31)

busker	living statue
concert hall	mural
exhibition	painting
gallery	portrait painter
graffiti	sculpture
juggler	

1 Look at the words in the box. Choose a word. Don't tell your partner. Describe the word. Can your partner guess what it is?

You can hear an orchestra play here.

Instruments (page 34)

banjo	flute	piano	violin
cello	guitar	recorder	trumpet
clarinet	keyboards	saxophone	tambourine
drums	mouth organ		

1 Look at the words in the box. Match them to the correct musical family. Which instrument doesn't fit into any family?

wind	string	percussion

2 Talk to your partner about instruments you play or have tried. Which is your favourite?

 Explore collocations (page 32)

good at	post online
make money	take photos
passionate about	work hard

1 Look at the words in the box. Match them to the correct collocation pattern.

adjective + preposition	verb + noun	verb + adverb
good at		

2 Can you add three more words to the chart that collocate with any of the adjectives, prepositions, verbs or nouns?

 Explore phrasal verbs with *up* (page 37)

dress up	pick up	tidy up
light up	set up	show up

1 Look at the words in the box. Write an example sentence for three of the phrasal verbs.

My mum always asks me to tidy up my bedroom.

2 Look at the verbs below. Which verb doesn't go with *up* to make a phrasal verb? Can you work out what the preposition is? Use a dictionary to check the meanings.

look	fall	give
set	add	catch
get	turn	grow

up	down
dress up	*get down*
show up	*turn down*

 Study tip

Write phrasal verbs in sets.

Vocabulary Bank

 Jog your memory!

1 Cover the rest of the page. How many expressions with *go* and phrasal verbs can you remember?

Expressions with *go* (page 41)

a guided tour	sailing
a safari	skiing
a school exchange	summer camp
a theme park	trekking
climbing	

1 Look at the words and phrases in the box. Match them with the correct heading.

go	go on	go to

2 Compare your list with your partner. Talk about which of the activities you like doing or have done.

I go on a summer camp every year. I really enjoy it.
We went trekking in the mountains last year.

Phrasal verbs (page 44)

chill	back
come	off
find	out
look	out
pick	round
set	up

1 Turn to page 44. Look at the phrasal verbs for one minute.

2 Can you remember them all? Match the words in the box to make phrasal verbs.

 Explore interesting adjectives (page 47)

important	spectacular
amazing	popular
striking	

1 Look again at page 47. What additional adjective is used to describe the tattoos?

2 Write a sentence to show the meaning of each adjective.
I have got some really important exams next week.

amaze (v) amazing (adj)
amazingly (adv)

Study tip

Write other forms of words in your vocabulary notebook to help extend your vocabulary.

Vocabulary Bank

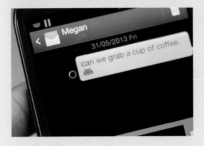

 Jog your memory!

1 Cover the rest of the page. How many communication words can you remember?

Communication (page 53)

blog post	phone call
chatting	Skype™
email	text message
social media post	Tweet
forum	

1 Look at the words in the box. Where can you …

- see pictures and information about your friends?
- see and talk to someone?
- only use 140 characters to say what you want?
- read about someone's thoughts, opinions or experiences?
- talk about a subject with other people online?

Communication verbs (page 56)

argue	gossip
boast	joke
complain	shout
criticise	whisper

1 Look at the words in the box. Write sentences about each verb.

I often argue with my sister.

2 Work with a partner. Read your sentences but don't say the verb. Your partner guesses the verb.

You should …. in the library. (whisper)

 Explore communication collocations (page 54)

digital	friends
face-	generation
social	network sites
status	to-face
virtual	update

1 Look at the words in the boxes. Match them to make collocations.

digital generation

2 Look at the text on page 54. Can you complete three more collocations?

- a …. media
- b online ….
- c …. forum

 Explore phrasal verbs (page 59)

go up
get by
keep on
come into use
turn into

1 Look at the phrasal verbs in the box. Work with a partner and write an example sentence for each one.

2 Check your answers on page 59. Correct any sentences that are wrong.

 Study tip

Sort words in your vocabulary book by collocations.

Vocabulary Bank

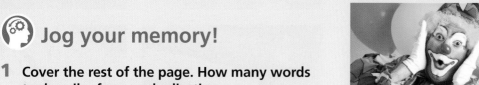

Jog your memory!

1 Cover the rest of the page. How many words to describe fears and adjectives can you remember?

Fears (page 63)

| birds | flying | insects | snakes |
| clowns | heights | lifts | the dark |

1 Look at the words in the box. Write the fears in the correct column.

animals	people	things
birds		

2 Can you add three more fears to the list?

-ed and -ing adjectives (page 66)

bored / boring	excited / exciting
terrified / terrifying	tired / tiring
interested / interesting	worried / worrying

1 Look at the words in the box. Write six sentences. Use three -ing adjectives and three -ed adjectives.

That film was really boring. I'm terrified of spiders.

Explore prepositional phrases (page 64)

embarrassed ....
share something .... someone
terrified ....
think ....
worried ....

1 Look at the words in the box. Write the correct preposition (*of, about* or *with*) to make prepositional phrases.

2 Do these words go with *about* or *of*? Which two words match both *about* and *of*?

| afraid | talk | fear | think |
| nightmare | scared | phobia | excited |

3 Write four sentences about yourself.
I always get excited about parties.

Explore opposite adjectives (page 69)

bad	dangerous
modern	good
safe	lucky
sensible	old
unlucky	silly
unsuccessful	successful

1 Look at the words in boxes. Match the opposite adjectives.
bad/good

2 You can add *un-* to one more adjective to make it opposite. Which adjective is it? Can you think of any other adjectives that you can add the prefix *un-* to?

3 Choose four of the words. Write four sentences using the words.

unlucky, unsuccessful

Study tip

Write prefixes in a different colour.

Vocabulary Bank

 Jog your memory!

1 Cover the rest of the page. How many school words can you remember?

Life at school (page 75)

be	hand	wear	bullying	get
scream	write	cheat	get	

a uniform	in a test	on time
detention	in homework	or shout
good marks	lines	

1 Look at the words in the boxes. Match them to make phrases about life at school. There is one word which doesn't match anything. Which word is it?

2 Look back at page 75 and check your answers.

3 Talk to your partner. What happens in your school? Use the words in the box to discuss.

make and *do* (page 78)

a mess	a decision
a mistake	friends
a noise	something interesting
a phone call	the right thing
an exercise	your homework

1 Look at the words in the box. Match the words with the correct verbs.

make	do
a mess	

2 Look back at page 78 and check your answers.

3 Work with a partner. Test him/her. Close your books. Say a word. Your partner says the correct verb, *make* or *do.*

 Explore phrasal verbs (page 81)

find out	work out	try out
pick up	write out	

1 Look at the definitions on page 81 again. Write a sentence with each phrasal verb that is personal to you and shows its meaning.
I like finding out about other countries.
It's interesting.

2 Look at these phrasal verbs with *out* and *up.* Discuss their meaning with a partner. Use a dictionary to help you.

log out	go out	look up
drop out	grow up	hang up

 Study tip

Listen to music and watch films to help you learn new vocabulary. Remember to write new words in your vocabulary notebook.

Vocabulary Bank

 Jog your memory!

1 Cover the rest of the page. How many words to describe materials and energy issues can you remember?

Materials (page 85)

bricks	metal
cement	paper
cotton	plastic
glass	rubber
leather	wood

1 Look at the words in the box. Think about your house. Write an object you can find there for each type of material in the box.

bricks – my garden wall

2 Work with a partner. Take turns to read your descriptions and guess the material.

A: My favourite T-shirt!   B: Cotton?

Energy issues (page 88)

consume
leave on standby
reduce
save energy
switch off
turn down
waste

1 Turn to page 88. Look at the definitions again.

2 Can you remember them all? Give examples of what you do to save energy in your house.

I never leave the TV on standby.

 Explore phrasal verbs (page 91)

bring	*down*	knock	....
cut	....	put	....
keep	....		

1 Look at the verbs in the box. Write *down, on* or *up* to make a phrasal verb.

2 Check your answers on page 91. Can you think of an example sentence for each phrasal verb?

When they brought down the price of the laptop, I had enough money to buy it.

consume (verb) [T]
/kənˈsjuːm/
to use fuel, energy or time, especially in large amounts

 Study tip

Use a dictionary to check how words are spelt, the pronunciation and the type of word it is.

Biology Global warming

1 **Work with a partner. Answer the questions about the greenhouse effect.**

1 What is the 'greenhouse effect'?
2 Which gases cause the greenhouse effect?
3 What is a greenhouse?
4 How does a greenhouse work?

2 **Read the texts (a–d) and match the questions in Exercise 1.**

3 🔊 **1.51** **Listen and check.**

a A greenhouse is a structure made of glass or plastic. Farmers and gardeners use them for growing plants in.

b A greenhouse changes sunlight into heat. The Sun's radiation goes through the glass or plastic walls and roof as light. This heats up the air, then the walls and roof keep the heat inside.

c When we talk about the greenhouse effect, we mean the planet is working like a greenhouse. The Sun's **radiation** enters the Earth's atmosphere and heats up the Earth's surface. Thermal, **infra-red radiation** comes from the Earth's surface, but **gases** in the atmosphere don't allow it all to escape. In fact, they reflect it back at the Earth like the walls and roof of a greenhouse. This causes what scientists call 'global warming'.

d Different gases cause the greenhouse effect. The most common are water vapour, carbon dioxide (CO_2), methane, nitrous oxide and ozone. All of these gases exist naturally in our environment. Without them, the Earth would be too cold to support life – but too much of them can make temperatures rise. In fact, nowadays, the average global surface temperature is almost a degree higher than it was a hundred years ago.

4 **Match the words in bold from the text to the numbers in the diagram.**

5 **Work with a partner. What problems does global warming cause? Make a list.**

6 **Read the information and check your answers from Exercise 5.**

Higher temperatures are changing our environment. The Polar ice caps are melting and causing sea levels to rise. This produces floods in coastal areas and also affects ecosystems in the world's oceans and seas. It can cause extreme weather conditions, too – violent storms and hurricanes, for example. And it doesn't stop there. The higher temperatures make water evaporate from the land more quickly. This causes water loss and can turn good land into deserts. This desertification makes land more difficult to farm, and, of course, affects wildlife.

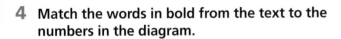

Your turn

7 **Work with a partner. Make a list of things you can do at home to reduce the amount of CO_2 you produce. Then compare your list with another pair.**

Learn about the greenhouse effect.
● Why is the Earth getting hotter?
● What happens to the oceans?
● What happens to the water?

Discovery EDUCATION™

1.4 Hot topics

2 CLIL

P.E. Avoiding sports injuries

1 Work with a partner. Match the body parts to the words in the box.

> joints   muscles   ~~ligaments~~
> shoulder   ankle   knee

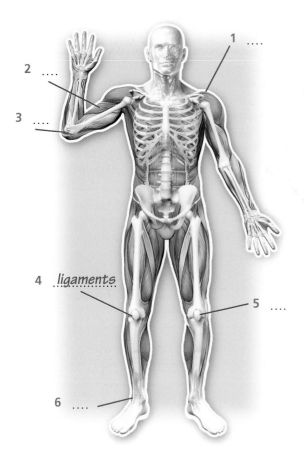

1 ....
2 ....
3 ....
4 _ligaments_
5 ....
6 ....

2 Complete the introduction giving advice on avoiding sports injuries with words from Exercise 1.

> Playing sports and taking exercise can be fun and can help you stay healthy, but anyone can get injured. Sports injuries can affect all parts of the body, but most injuries affect [1] ...., [2] .... and [3] .... Certain types of sport can affect different parts of the body. Tennis players often have [4] ... problems, for example, and people who go jogging can have problems with [5] .... and [6] .... .

3 🔊 **1.52** Listen and check.

4 🔊 **1.53** Complete the advice with the words in the box. Then listen and check.

> injuries   ~~blood flow~~   stiff   pain   muscles   equipment

We can avoid most problems by following these simple guidelines.

1 Prepare properly for sport. Warm-up exercises before doing sport increase the [1] _blood flow_ to the [2] .... and make them more flexible.

2 Cooling down is important, too. It stops you feeling [3] .... the next day.

3 Get the right [4] .... Using the wrong type of sports shoes or a tennis racquet of the wrong weight can cause problems.

4 Be careful with technique and posture. Talking to experienced sports people about this can help you avoid unnecessary [5] ....

5 If you feel [6] .... during exercise, it's a sign that there's a problem, so stop!

6 Don't start doing sport again too soon after an injury. Wait for the pain to go first. Doing sport too soon after an injury can make it worse.

Your turn

5 Work with a partner. Choose a sport. Make a leaflet explaining how to avoid injury in a sport.

Learn about helping someone.
- What does Bear Grylls do first?
- Why doesn't his mobile phone work?
- How does Bear pull Jesse up the mountain?

2.4 Mountain rescue

Art Perspective

1 Work with a partner. Look at the paintings. Can you see anything unusual about them?

2 🔊 **1.54** Read the information about perspective. Check your ideas about the paintings.

In the past, pictures of people, places and things didn't look like they do in real life. They looked flat and out of proportion. In the 13th century, artists began to produce life-like images by giving their pictures perspective.

When we look at things around us, they are three dimensional (3D) – they have volume and depth. An artist uses perspective to create a representation on a two dimensional (2D) piece of paper or canvas of how we see things in real life with space, distance and depth between the various objects.

Foreshortening objects gives the impression of perspective. The artist reduces the size of objects in a picture as they follow the viewer's line of sight into the distance. These lines converge in vanishing points on the viewer's horizon and the objects become too small to see. This makes parts of the image appear far away in the background or close to the viewer in the foreground.

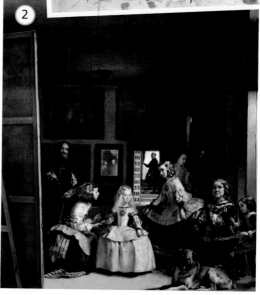

3 Read the information again and answer the questions.
1 When did artists start to use perspective?
2 What were pictures like before that?
3 What does an artist use perspective for?
4 How does an artist show perspective?
5 What happens to objects close to the vanishing point?

4 🔊 **1.55** Listen to a teacher and students in an art class. Which of the following do they mention?
- lines of sight
- shadow
- middle ground
- landscape
- vanishing point
- background
- three dimensional
- foreshortening

5 Work with a partner. Match the paintings with the titles and artists. Use the words in Exercise 4 to discuss them.
a *Las Meninas,* 1656, Diego Velázquez
b *Paris Street, Rainy day,* 1877, Gustave Caillebotte

Your turn

6 Choose a painting. Use the Internet to find out information about it.
Think about …
… who painted it and when.
… the use of perspective in the painting.
… what you like/don't like about the painting.
Share your ideas in class.

Learn about renaissance painters.
- Where did the renaissance begin?
- What did the renaissance painters want to do?
- Why did they want to do this?

⊙Discovery
EDUCATION™

3.4 Art in perspective

Geography Time zones

1 **Work with a partner. Complete the diagram with the parallels and meridians (1–4).**

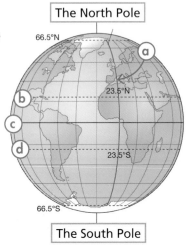

The North Pole

66.5°N

a

23.5°N

b

c

d

23.5°S

66.5°S

The South Pole

1 The Equator
2 The Tropic of Cancer
3 The Tropic of Capricorn
4 The Prime/Greenwich Meridian

2 🔊 **1.56** **Read the information about parallels and meridians. Check your answers to Exercise 1.**

THE EARTH AND ITS
IMAGINARY LINES

Lines of latitude or parallels are horizontal lines dividing the Earth's surface. The line of latitude in the centre of the sphere is called the Equator. The Equator divides the globe into two hemispheres. Anything above the Equator is in the northern hemisphere and anything below is in the southern hemisphere.

Coordinates specify a north-south position on the Earth's surface, ranging from 0 degrees on the equator to 90 degrees at the poles. The North Pole is at 90 degrees north, and the South Pole is at 90 degrees south.

The Tropic of Cancer and The Tropic of Capricorn are two other important parallels. The Tropic of Cancer is above the Equator at 23.5 degrees north and the Tropic of Capricorn is below the Equator at 23.5 degrees south. These two lines of latitude mark the northern and southern limits of what is known as the tropics.

Lines of longitude or meridians are the vertical lines dividing the Earth's surface. The line of longitude passing through the Royal Observatory at Greenwich, near London, is the Prime Meridian. It's the international zero-longitude reference line. Places to the east of the Prime Meridian are in the eastern hemisphere, and places to the west are in the western hemisphere.

3 🔊 **1.57** **Complete the information about time zones with the words and phrases in the box. Then listen and check.**

> add   daylight   direction   forward
> thirty   twenty-four

Time zones

There are [1] .... time zones in the world.

Most of the time zones are one hour divisions, but a few are [2] .... or forty-five minutes.

Some higher latitude countries use [3] .... saving time. In the autumn, the clocks are put back, and in the spring the clocks are put [4] .....

To calculate the time in a different time zone, you have to add or subtract hours depending on the [5] .... you are going. If you are going east, you need to [6] .... hours. If you are going west, you need to subtract them.

Your turn

4 **Ask and answer with your partner.**

1 What hemisphere do you live in?
2 Do you live closer to the Tropic of Cancer or the Tropic of Capricorn?
3 If you live in London and travel to New York, would you need to put your watch back or forward?

Learn about the world.

- What two different things can we use to look at the world?
- Where is Houston?
- Where is it always cold?

▶ ◉**Discovery** EDUCATION™

4.4 **Where in the world?**

Technology Early written communication

1 Work with a partner Answer the questions.

- When did people start writing?
- How did the ancient Egyptians write?
- Where does the word 'alphabet' come from?

2 🔊 **2.44 Read the text and check your ideas.**

Our earliest human ancestors first stood on two legs around 6 million years ago. But it was the ability to share information which set our ancestors apart from the rest of the animals. Communication remained very limited until our closest ancestor, Homo erectus, appeared about 1.8 million years ago. But it was only 6,000 years ago, with Homo sapiens, that any form of writing came into existence.

The earliest forms of writing were logographic and used symbols (logograms) to represent things. The most famous of these old forms of writing is hieroglyphics. The Ancient Egyptians either carved or painted hieroglyphs on stone. However, they also had two other forms of writing, called hieratic and demotic. They wrote onto papyrus, a form of paper, or cloth with ink or paint. We know a lot about hieroglyphic writing because of the Rosetta Stone. This is an ancient stone slab with the same message written in hieroglyphics, demotic and Ancient Greek.

Alphabetic writing systems use marks which represent sounds. Ancient Greek was the first complete alphabet and represented both consonant and vowel sounds. In fact, the word alphabet comes from the first two Greek letters, alpha and beta. It was a unique invention and many different languages now use some form of complete alphabet. English uses the Roman alphabet, which the Romans adapted from the ancient Greek.

3 Read the text again. Are the sentences true or false? Correct the false ones.

1 Homo erectus used a logographic writing system.
2 The ancient Egyptians had three forms of writing.
3 The Egyptians carved hieroglyphs into stone.
4 The Ancient Greek alphabet only represented consonant sounds.
5 The Romans adapted their alphabet from hieroglyphics.

4 Complete the text with the words in the box.

> logograms x2   spoken   alphabets
> logographic   alphabetic   pronunciation

Hieroglyphics was a [1].... system of writing. It used [2]... to represent objects and actions. Because they were not related to [3]...., different languages could use the same [4].....
[5].... systems of writing use marks to represent sounds of the [6]... language so different languages might use the same [7].... but spelling and grammar will be different.

5 🔊 **2.45 Listen to a linguist talking about reading and writing. What subjects does he talk about?**

a The Romans
b dangerous animals
c books for wealthy people
d cheap books
e Internet blogs

Your turn

6 Work with a partner and write a short message. Write the message using only pictures. Show your message to the rest of the class to see if they can work it out.

Learn about hieroglyphics.

- What has the archaeologist come to see?
- How long has the skeleton been there?
- Why was the sandal strap important to Egyptians?

▶ **Discovery** EDUCATION™

5.4 Pictures with meaning

Geography Living in a global city

1 Work with a partner. Look at the photos. Which cities are they? Make a list of the advantages of living in a city.

2 🔊 **2.46** Read the information about cities. Are any of your ideas from Exercise 1 mentioned?

A city is a large, densely populated area with a high concentration of buildings and an infrastructure of services and facilities. Unlike rural areas, the majority of economic activities in cities is in manufacturing or services, like public administration, transport, health care and entertainment.

Cities can be classified in different ways. We can call them global, governmental, industrial or tourist, according to their main activity. Global cities usually combine aspects of all types, but their main importance is in the global economy.

As well as being important world economic centres, most global cities share various features. They usually have large cosmopolitan populations; they have the headquarters of multinational companies and they have cultural centres with important museums, art galleries and universities. Global cities usually have advanced public transport systems and a major airport. In general, global cities have an active influence on world events.

3 Read the information again and complete the following summary.

> The economies of most cities are based on
> ¹*manufacturing* and ² .... Services include
> public administration, health care, ³ ....
> and ⁴ ....
> Global cities are important world ⁵ .... centres.
> They have large ⁶ .... populations. ⁷ .... have
> their headquarters there. They are cultural
> centres with ⁸ ...., art galleries and ⁹ .....

4 🔊 **2.47** Listen and check.

Your turn

5 Work with a partner. One of you look at Photo 1, the other at Photo 2. Make a list of the advantages of living in this place.

6 Discuss the advantages and disadvantages of living in the place in your photo.

Learn about Russian cities.
- What advantages are there for living in the countryside?
- How many people live in Moscow?
- What are people proud of in St Petersburg?

Discovery EDUCATION™

6.4 City or country?

CLIL

Technology Social media

1 Work with a partner. Answer the questions.

1 What social media sites do you use?
2 In what ways can social media be useful for teenagers?

2 🔊 2.48 Read the information about teenagers and social media. Check your ideas from Exercise 1.

Using **social media** can be a good thing.

Social media sites and networking can:

– improve communication between teenagers and their teachers, because they are available at all times from almost anywhere.
– encourage teenagers to interact with each other, share ideas and be creative by letting people communicate in different ways.
– help develop relationships with real people. They can help shy teenagers find friends who follow the same singers, sports stars and so on, and feel part of a group.
– expose teenagers to different viewpoints and new ideas through a wide variety of online communities.
– help teenagers get better at analysing and selecting important information. There's a lot of information on social media pages, so users become good at finding key information quickly.
– help familiarise students with new technologies. Social media sites are constantly changing – to stay up to date, teenagers have to learn new ways of using them.
– help students enter the world of work. Professional networking sites like LinkedIn™ can help people find out about different professions and job offers.

3 Read the text again. Which three benefits do you think are the most important? Compare with a partner.

4 🔊 2.49 Listen to three teenagers on a radio phone-in. Match the speakers to the social media they talk about.

John	a	can organise images and create collections on Pinterest
Sarah		
Mark	b	likes Myspace because it's good for sharing music.
	c	uses Facebook to exchange messages and photos.
	d	likes Twitter because messages are short.

Your turn

5 Ask and answer with your partner.

1 What's your favourite social media site?
2 What do you like about it?
3 Is there anything you don't like about it?

Learn about being safe online.
● How can you be sure who you are talking to online?
● What does a criminal need to get a credit card?
● What should you do with messages from people you don't know?

▶ **●DISCOVERY** EDUCATION™

7.4 Be safe online

121

Chemistry Renewable energy

1 Work with a partner. Look at the photos. How many sources of renewable energy can you think of?

2 🔊 **2.50** Read the information about sources of energy. Check your answers from Exercise 1.

At the moment we get about 70% of our energy from fossil fuels like oil, coal and natural gas, but there are two main problems with this. Firstly, they release CO_2 when we burn them and secondly, they take millions of years to form and the supply is limited.

Fossil fuels are not the only sources of energy. Alternative energy is energy generated from any source other than 'traditional' fossil fuels and which doesn't damage our environment. The sun (solar energy), wind (eolic energy), water (hydroelectric energy) and tides and waves (tidal and wave power) are all alternative energy sources. They are also called renewable energy because they won't run out or sustainable energy because we can use it now without affecting the supply in the future.

There are other sources of energy such as biofuel and nuclear power, but these are not strictly alternative energy sources. Biofuel is a term that includes a wide variety of fuels obtained from biomass (carbon-based biological material, usually plants), so it releases CO_2 in the same way as fossil fuels. Nuclear power doesn't produce CO_2, but it does produce waste which can stay toxic for 240,000 years.

Climate change and global warming, together with high oil prices and the risk of nuclear contamination, are making renewable energy sources more attractive. The production of alternative energy is growing very rapidly. It is estimated that 16% of all energy now comes from renewable resources.

3 Read the text again. Match the words in the box with the definitions.

> sustainable energy   renewable energy
> alternative energy   fossil fuels   biofuel

1 .... comes from sources that do not damage the environment.
2 .... comes from sources that do not run out.
3 .... gives us energy without affecting the supply in the future.
4 .... comes from material like plants.
5 .... are formed over millions of years from the remains of plants and animals.

4 Work with a partner. Answer the quiz questions about energy sources.

1 How much of the energy used by TVs is used while they're on standby?
A 10%   C 60%
B 35%   D 85%

2 How long can a game console run for if you recycle one aluminium can?
A 30 minutes   C 2 hours
B 1 hour   D 10 hours

3 Biodiesel is a kind of biofuel used in diesel engines. Which of these things CAN'T it be made from?
A coconuts   C potatoes
B used cooking oil   D sunflower seeds

4 How much of the world's electricity does the Sun provide every 15 minutes?
A Enough for three years.   C Enough for a day.
B Enough for a year.   D Enough for a month.

5 🔊 **2.51** Listen and check.

Your turn

6 Work with a partner. Make a poster to encourage students in your school to recycle and save energy. Follow the steps below.
- Decide together what information to put on your poster.
- Find photos and pictures to illustrate the information.
- Present your poster to your class.
- Vote on the class's favourite poster.

Learn about electric cars.
- Which countries are producing electric cars?
- What is Kevin's goal?
- Where are car batteries made?

Discovery EDUCATION™

8.4 Driving into the future

Project 1

An unusual hobby poster

PARKOUR

take to the streets!

WHAT IS IT?
Parkour comes from military training and involves running, jumping and climbing over obstacles outdoors. It can also involve moving on your hands and feet like a cat. It is a non-competitive activity which started in France in the 1980s and became popular through documentaries, films like *Casino Royale* (a James Bond movie) and TV advertisements. People who do the sport are called traceurs (for boys) or traceuses (for girls).

WHAT DO YOU NEED?
Nothing! You don't have to use any special equipment. Traceurs usually wear casual, sporty clothes like T-shirts, tracksuit bottoms and running shoes.

WHERE CAN YOU DO IT?
The best thing about parkour is that you can do it anywhere! Traceurs use urban and rural areas in places like parks, playgrounds, gyms and offices.

HOW CAN YOU DO IT?
Start by following the steps below:
1. Find somewhere safe like a park or a garden.
2. Practise running and jumping to help improve your balance.
3. Then try to jump backwards or do cartwheels (when you stand on your hands and land on your feet).
4. Finally, try to do this from a small height and land on the ground. And this is parkour!

Prepare

2 **Work in groups of three or four. Choose an unusual hobby that is popular with teenagers in your country. Use the Internet, books or magazines to find information about it. Find out about …**

- where it comes from.
- what you need.
- where you can do it.
- how to do it.

3 **Find photos or draw pictures of the activity. Make a poster with the photos and the information about it.**

Present

4 **In your groups present your poster to the rest of the class. Then ask them questions about the hobby. Can they remember all the important facts?**

Look

1 **Read the poster. Answer the following questions.**

1 Which actions does parkour involve?
2 When and where did it start?
3 How did it become popular?
4 What do traceurs wear?
5 Where can you do it?
6 Name two parkour movements from the text.

Project 2

A magazine article

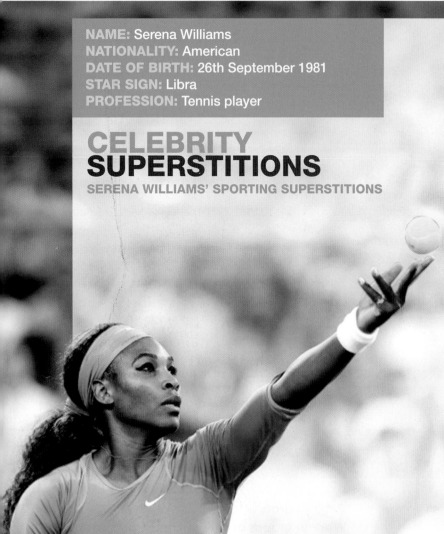

NAME: Serena Williams
NATIONALITY: American
DATE OF BIRTH: 26th September 1981
STAR SIGN: Libra
PROFESSION: Tennis player

CELEBRITY SUPERSTITIONS
SERENA WILLIAMS' SPORTING SUPERSTITIONS

1 ....
Serena is a famous American tennis player who has won many titles including Wimbledon, the French Open and the US Open. She has also been Olympic Singles and Doubles Champion. Serena is famous for being very competitive.

2 ....
Serena believes following special routines is the secret of her success. So she always:
- brings her shower sandals to the court.
- ties her shoelaces in a special way.
- bounces the ball five times before her first serve and two before the second.
- wears the same pair of socks for a whole tournament.

3 ....
Serena is always going to repeat this procedure to guarantee victory. She believes that she has lost matches because she has not followed those routines correctly.

4 ....
It is difficult to know how much this belief affect her performance on court – maybe there is som truth to this. After all, she is the most successfu female tennis player of all time. For all the tennis players reading this, now you know what to do to improve your game. How many times you choose to bounce the ball is up to you!

Look

1 Read the text. Then cover the text and try to remember four things that Serena does to win the match. Compare your ideas with a partner.

2 Match the headings with the paragraphs.
- a Why she follows the superstition
- b Conclusion
- c Background information
- d What the superstition is

Prepare

3 Work in groups of three or four. Choose a famous celebrity. Use the Internet, books or magazines to find information about him/her. Find out about …
- his/her career.
- what he/she has won.
- any superstitions he/she has.

Present

4 Display the magazine article on the wall in your classroom. Ask your classmates to read it. Have a class vote to choose the strangest celebrity superstition.

An information leaflet

GREEN JEWELLERY

1 ....

This is a piece of recycled jewellery that your friends won't have. It is called a necklace and you wear it round your neck. It comes in different sizes and colours so you can pick your favourite one.

2 ....

Lego is a company that makes small, plastic building blocks for children. They put the pieces together to make cars, aeroplanes, houses and cities. Well, this necklace was made with plastic Lego pieces. In the past they were used for making Lego houses, boats, planes and castles. Now you can wear them on your body as jewellery like earrings, necklaces and bracelets.

3 ....

Jewellery is usually made from metal that is mined from the earth and this damages the environment. However, this jewellery is made with plastic from children's old toys. Plastic has a long life so if you don't reuse it, it will stay on a rubbish dump for the next four hundred years!

4 ....

You don't have to spend money to be fashionable. Why not try to make some jewellery at home? Use old toys, household objects and some elastic. Be creative and you can make your own designs for much less money.

Look

1 Match the words in the box with the pictures.

> bracelet   earring   jewellery   necklace

2 Read the text. Match the questions with the paragraphs.

a   What can you make?
b   What is it made of?
c   Why is it the best 'green' product?
d   What is it?

Prepare

3 Work in groups of three or four. Use the Internet to find examples of recycled products based on things you can find in your home. Choose your favourite one and make notes about it. Use the questions in Exercise 2 to help you.

4 Make an information leaflet on your favourite recycled product. Use photos or draw a picture of the product and the information in Exercise 3. Then think of a title which relates to the product and its use.

Present

5 Display the leaflet on the wall in your classroom. Ask your classmates to read it. Then test their memory using the questions in Exercise 2. Have a class vote to choose the best 'green' product.

Irregular verbs

infinitive	past simple	past participle
be	was/were	been
become	became	become
begin	began	begun
break	broke	broken
build	built	built
buy	bought	bought
catch	caught	caught
choose	chose	chosen
come	came	come
do	did	done
drink	drank	drunk
drive	drove	driven
eat	ate	eaten
fall	fell	fallen
feed	fed	fed
feel	felt	felt
find	found	found
fly	flew	flown
get	got	got
give	gave	given
go	went	gone
have	had	had
hear	heard	heard
keep	kept	kept
know	knew	known
learn	learnt/learned	learnt/learned
leave	left	left
lose	lost	lost
make	made	made
meet	met	met
pay	paid	paid
put	put	put
read	read	read
run	ran	run
say	said	said
see	saw	seen
send	sent	sent
sit	sat	sat
sleep	slept	slept
speak	spoke	spoken
spend	spent	spent
swim	swam	swum
take	took	taken
teach	taught	taught
tell	told	told
think	thought	thought
wear	wore	worn
win	won	won
write	wrote	written

Phonemic symbols

consonants

/p/	pencil
/b/	bag
/t/	town
/d/	day
/tʃ/	cheese
/dʒ/	juice
/k/	cake
/g/	get
/f/	food
/v/	very
/θ/	Thursday
/ð/	that
/s/	speak
/z/	zebra
/ʃ/	shoe
/ʒ/	usually
/m/	mum
/n/	name
/ŋ/	sing
/h/	house
/l/	like
/r/	red
/w/	water
/j/	you

vowels

/i:/	see
/ɪ/	sit
/ʊ/	book
/u:/	zoo
/e/	pen
/ə/	teacher
/ɜ:/	bird
/ɔ:/	boring
/æ/	that
/ʌ/	run
/ɑ:/	car
/ɒ/	lost

diphthongs

/eɪ/	say
/ɪə/	hear
/ʊə/	pure
/ɔɪ/	enjoy
/əʊ/	know
/eə/	chair
/aɪ/	buy
/aʊ/	now

Thanks and acknowledgements

The authors and publishers would like to thank all the teachers and consultants who have contributed to the development of this course, in particular:

Argentina: Fernando Armesto; Natalia Bitar; Verónica Borrás; Leonor Corradi ; Paz Moltrasio; Diana Ogando; Brazil: Dalmo Carvalho; Roberto Costa; Sônia M. B. Leites; Gloria Paz; Litany Pires Ribeiro; Christina Riego; Renata Condi de Souza; Elizabeth White; Chile: Magdalena Aldunate; M. Cristina Darraidou Diaz; Valentina Donoso; Ana María Páez Jofrré; Ricardo Contreras Marambio; Claudia Ottone; Maria Elena Ramirez; Jacqueline Rondon; Alicia Paez Ubilla; Colombia: Luz Amparo Bautista; Sonia Ruiz Hernández; Sandra Jara; Fabian Jimenez; Bibiana Andrea Piñeros Merizalde; Lucero Amparo Bernal Nieto; Olga Olarte; Bibiana Piñeros; Emelis Rambut; Sonia Ruíz; Poland: Anna Bylicka; Russia: Natalya Melchenkova; Irina Polyakova; Svetlana Suchkova; Irina Vayserberg; Turkey: Ali Bilgin; Angela Çakır; Shirley Nuttal; Cinla Sezgin; Mujgan Yesiloglu

The publishers are grateful to the following for permission to reproduce copyright photographs and material:
Cover: Alamy/©Martin Strimska; Back cover: Shutterstock Images/fluke samed; p. 6 (BR): Shutterstock Images/ Prometheus72; p. 6 (TL): Alamy/©Stockbroker; p. 7 (TL): Shutterstock Images/Jacek Chabraszewski; p. 7 (TC): Shutterstock Images/scyther5; p. 7 (BC): Shutterstock Images/Ervin Monn; p. 8 (B/G): Getty Images/Stone; p. 9 (a): Shutterstock Images/Tom Wang; p. 9 (b): Shutterstock Images/fluke samed; p. 9 (c): Alamy/©blickwinkel; p. 9 (d): Alamy/©David R. Frazier Photolibrary Inc.; p. 9 (e): Shutterstock Images/egd; p. 9 (f): Shutterstock Images/Richard Whitcombe; p. 9 (g): Shutterstock Images/Igumnova Irina; p. 9 (h): Shutterstock Images/James BO Insogna; p. 10 (B): Alamy/©RIA Novosti; p. 10 (BC): Alamy/©RIA Novosti; p. 11 (TR): Alamy/©Kumar Sriskandan; p. 12-13 (B/G): Alamy/©Paul Mayall Australia; p. 14 (B/G T): Alamy/©Plinthpics; p. 14 (BR): Alamy/©Ben Pipe; p. 14 (C): Alamy/©Images of Africa Photobank; p. 14 (TR): Alamy/©Trish Ainslie; p. 14-15 (B/G): Alamy/©Chris Howarth/South Atlantic; p. 16 (TR): Alamy/©Ellen Isaacs; p. 16 (BR): Alamy/© VIEW Pictures Ltd/; p. 17 (TR): Alamy/©Tim Graham; p. 17 (BR): Shutterstock Images/Burro; p. 18 (B/G): Corbis/2/Arctic-Images/Ocean; p. 19 (a): Alamy/©Tetra Images; p. 19 (b): Alamy/©Kuttig - People; p. 19 (c): Alamy/©Justin Kase zsixz; p. 19 (d): Shutterstock Images/Masson; p. 19 (e): Shutterstock Images/kuznetcov_konstantin; p. 19 (f): Superstock/age footstock; p. 19 (g): Getty Images/Image Source; p. 19 (h): REX/Phanie/Garo; p. 20 (T): Getty Images/Susanne Walstrom/Johner Images; p. 22 (TR): Shutterstock Images/bullet74; p. 22 (BR): Alamy/©The Art Archive; p. 23 (BC): Shutterstock Images/Helder Almeida; p. 24 (T): Alamy/©Paul Doyle; p. 24 (CR): Alamy/©ZUMA Press Inc.; p. 25 (B/G): Alamy/©Ulrich Doering; p. 25 (BL): Alamy/©LondonPhotos - Homer Sykes; p. 26 (BL): Alamy/©Kumar Sriskandan; p. 26 (CR): Alamy/©Blend Images; p. 27 (TL): Getty Images/Cavan Images/Taxi; p. 27 (TC): Getty Images/Steve Mason/Photodisc; p. 27 (CL): Shutterstock Images/Anna Jurkovska; p. 30 (B/G): Alamy/©Nikreates; p. 31 (a): Alamy/©Ian Francis; p. 31 (b): Alamy/©Arco Images GmbH; p. 31 (c): Alamy/©JOHN KELLERMAN; p. 31 (d): Alamy/©Andrew Aitchison; p. 31 (e): Corbis/ Sylvain Sonnet; p. 31 (f): Alamy/©eddie linssen; p. 31 (g): Alamy/©Ferenc Szelepcsenyi; p. 31 (h): Getty Images/Getty Images Sport/Andy Lyons; p. 31 (i): Alamy/©Michele and Tom Grimm; p. 31 (j): Alamy/©Artepics; p. 32 (BL): Alamy/©LOOK Die Bildagentur der Fotografen GmbH; p. 33 (TR): Corbis/ Bernd Kammerer/dpa; p. 33 (BL): Getty Images/Maartje Van Caspel; p. 34 (1): Shutterstock Images/Andrey_Popov; p. 34 (2): Shutterstock Images/mphot; p. 34 (3): Shutterstock Images/Vereshchagin Dmitry; p. 34 (4): Shutterstock Images/Redkaya; p. 34 (5): Shutterstock Images/Furtseff; p. 34 (6): Shutterstock Images/vvoe; p. 34 (7): Shutterstock Images/grigiomedio; p. 34 (8): Shutterstock Images/J. Helgason; p. 34 (9): Shutterstock Images/Dario Sabljak; p. 34 (10): Shutterstock Images/Chromakey; p. 34 (11): Shutterstock Images/Visun Khankasem; p. 34 (12): Shutterstock Images/Mike Braune; p. 34 (13): Shutterstock Images/ Jouke van Keulen; p. 34 (14): Alamy/©Aki; p. 34 (TR): Alamy/©i stage; p. 36 (a): Alamy/©Richard Ellis; p. 36 (b): Alamy/©Stephen Chung; p. 36 (c): Alamy/©Universal Images Group Limited; p. 37 (C): REX/KeystoneUSA-ZUMA; p. 37 (CR): Getty Images/r e y . t o r r e s/Moment Open; p. 37 (BR): Alamy/©ZUMA Press, Inc.; p. 38 (CL): Corbis/Dirk Lindner; p. 39 (TC): Alamy/©Gari Wyn Williams; p. 39 (TL): Alamy/©david pearson; p. 40 (B/G): Alamy/©Michael Jones/Alaska Stock; p. 41 (a): ©CUP/Mark Bassett; p. 41 (b): Alamy/©AugustSnow; p. 41 (c): Alamy/©Dmitry Burlakov; p. 41 (d): Getty Images/Ken Chernus/Taxi; p. 41 (e): Shutterstock Images/PhotoSky; p. 41 (f): Alamy/©ZUMA Press, Inc.; p. 41 (g): Shutterstock Images/wavebreakmedia; p. 41 (h): Shutterstock Images/Johnny Adolphson; p. 41 (i): Shutterstock Images/ Stephen B. Goodwin; p. 42 (BC): Alamy/©ianmurray; p. 42 (BR): Alamy/©Mar Photographics; p. 44 (TL): Alamy/©Alibi Productions; p. 45 (CR): Alamy/©Purepix; p. 46 (TR): Shutterstock Images/Lev Kropotov; p. 46 (TC): Alamy/©Howard Davies; p. 46 (B/G): Shutterstock Images/Tooykrub; p. 47 (BR): Alamy/©Blaine Harrington III; p. 47 (TR): Alamy/©Allstar Picture Library; p. 47 (TC): Agefotostock/Stuart Blac; p. 48 (TL): Alamy/©Hemis; p. 48 (CR): Shutterstock Images/Strahil Dimitrov; p. 48 (BR): Alamy/©PhotoAlto; p. 49 (TR): Alamy/©Jochen Tack; p. 49 (TL): Alamy/©Wim Wiskerke; p. 50 (BR): Shutterstock Images/Gigi Peis; p. 51 (CR): Shutterstock Images/S.Borisov; p. 52 (B/G): Getty Images/Riou; p. 53 (a): Alamy/©Catchlight Visual Services; p. 53 (b): Alamy/©Buzzshotz; p. 53 (c): Alamy/©Anatolii Babii; p. 53 (d): Alamy/©IanDagnall Computing; p. 53 (e): Alamy/©NetPhotos; p. 53 (f): Alamy/©pumkinpie; p. 54-55 (b): Alamy/©Eric Audras; p. 56 (a): Shutterstock Images/Goran Djukanovic; p. 56 (b): Alamy/©John Powell/ Bubbles Photolibrary; p. 56 (c): Shutterstock Images/Tomasz Trojanowski; p. 56 (d): Alamy/©Blend Images; p. 57 (C): Alamy/©eye35.pix; p. 58 (T): Alamy/©Iain Masterton; p. 58 (CL): Alamy/©AKP Photos; p. 59 (BL): Alamy/©Top Photo/Asia Photo Connection/Henry Westheim Photography; p. 59 (BR): Shutterstock Images/Elena Elisseeva; p. 59 (TL): Alamy/©Bazza; p. 59 (BC): Alamy/©Liquid Light; p. 60 (TL): Alamy/©Valerie Garner; p. 60 (BL): Shutterstock Images/Deborah Kolb; p. 61 (TL): Shutterstock Images/Alexey Boldin; p. 62 (B/G): Getty Images/Jay P. Morgan; p. 63 (B/G): Shutterstock Images/Salajean; p. 63 (a): Alamy/©Robin Beckham/BEEPstock; p. 63 (b): Shutterstock Images/Jayakumar; p. 63 (c): Shutterstock Images/ Dmitrijs Bindemanis; p. 63 (d): Shutterstock Images/Matteo photos; p. 63 (e): Shutterstock Images/Lisa F. Young; p. 63 (f): Shutterstock Images/Jag_cz; p. 64 (BC): Shutterstock Images/Sarah2; p. 64 (TC): Alamy/©Radius Images; p. 64 (C): Shutterstock Images/juniart; p. 64 (B): Alamy/©Image Source; p. 65 (BL): /Shutterstock Images/Sergei A. Aleshi; p. 66 (L): Alamy/©Gunter Marx; p. 66 (C): Getty Images/Petri Artturi Asikainen/Folio Images; p. 66 (R): Superstock/Greer & Associates, Inc.; p. 67 (TL): Alamy/©Ruby; p. 68 (TR): Alamy/©Peter Horree; p. 68 (BL): Alamy/©Tuul/Robert Harding World Imagery; p. 68 (B/G): Alamy/©Dbimages; p. 69 (BL): Alamy/©Adrian Turner; p. 69 (CR): Alamy/©David Gee; p. 69 (CL): Shutterstock Images/Sergio Foto; p. 69 (TR): Alamy/©Photodreams1; p. 69 (TL): Alamy/©Felipe Rodriguez; p. 69 (BR): Shutterstock Images/Olga Selyutina; p. 69 (CT): Shutterstock Images/Erni; p. 70 (CL): Alamy/©James Nesterwitz;

p. 70 (CR): Getty Images/Echo/ultura; p. 70 (BR): Superstock/Marka; p. 71 (T): Getty Images/Elisabeth Schmitt/Moment Select; p. 72 (CR): Alamy/©Blue Jean Images; p. 73(TR): Shutterstock Images/cvrestan; p. 74 (B/G): Alamy/©Jennifer Podis/The Palm Beach Post/Zuma press; p. 75 (a): Alamy/©RubberBall; p. 75 (b): Alamy/©Westend61 GmbH; p. 75 (c): Corbis/©David Lefranc; p. 75 (d): Alamy/©imageBROKER; p. 75 (e): Shutterstock Images/BKMCphotography; p. 75 (f): Superstock/Image Source; p. 75 (g): Alamy/©Beyond Fotomedia GmbH; p. 75 (i): Getty Images/Silvia Otte/Taxi; p. 75 (f): Superstock/Image Source; p. 75 (h): Alamy/©Wavebreakmedia Ltd UC1; p. 76-77 (B): Alamy/©Riedmiller; p. 79 (CR): Alamy/©kt spencer march; p. 80 (TR): Getty Images/Inti St Clair/Digital Vision; p. 80 (TL): Alamy/©Ian Shaw; p. 80 (CR): Alamy/©Gregg Vignal; p. 81 (B/G): Shutterstock Images/oksana.perkins; p. 82 (TR): Alamy/©Image Source; p. 82 (CR): Alamy/©Tony Cordoza; p. 82 (BR): Alamy/©Marjorie Kamys Cotera/Bob Daemmrich Photography; p. 84 (B/G): Shutterstock Images/majeczka; p. 85 (a): Alamy/©imageBROKER; p. 85 (b): Alamy/©Steffen Hauser/botanikfoto; p. 85 (c): Q2A Media; p. 85 (d): Shutterstock Images/Sakarin Sawasdinaka; p. 85 (e): Q2A Media; p. 85 (f): Alamy/©Tom Merton/OJO Images Ltd; p. 85 (g): Q2A Media; p. 85 (h): Shutterstock Images/Kati Molin; p. 85 (i): Shutterstock Images/graphyx; p. 85 (j): Alamy/©Milena Boniek; p. 86 (CL): Alamy/©ZUMA Press; p. 86 (BL): Alamy/©Jay Goebel; p. 86-87 (B): Rex Features/Paul Cooper; p. 87 (TR): Corbis/Kirsten Neumann/Reuters; p. 88 (TL): Alamy/©Bubbles Photolibrary; p. 89 (B): Shutterstock Images/Subbotina Anna; p. 90 (TL): Alamy/©US Labor Department; p. 90 (BL): Alamy/©Craig Ruttle; p. 90 (T): Getty Images/Willoughby Owen; p. 91(CR): Shutterstock Images/Tchara; p. 91 (BR): Shutterstock Images/Daniel Schweinert; p. 91 (TR): Alamy/©Clynt Garnham Renewable Energy; p. 92 (BL): Superstock/imageBROKER; p. 92 (CR): Getty Images/Karl Lehmann/Lonely Planet Images; p. 92 (BR): Shutterstock Images/spwidoff; p. 93 (T): Alamy/©Todd Bannor; p. 93 (TR): Alamy/©Dave Porter; p. 95 (TR): Getty Images/Chris Schmidt; p. 107 (TR): Alamy/©Alaska Stock; p. 108 (TL): REX/Garo/Phanie; p. 108 (TR): Shutterstock Images/Masson; p. 108 (BR): Alamy/©Ted Foxx; p. 108 (BL): Alamy/©Blend Images; p. 109 (TR): Alamy/©Arco Images GmbH; p. 109 (BL): Alamy/©eddie linssen; p. 109 (TL): Alamy/©Alex Segre; p. 109 (BR): Shutterstock Images/koi88; p. 110 (TC): Getty Images/Ken Chernus; p. 110 (TR): Shutterstock Images/Stephen B. Goodwin; p. 110 (C): Shutterstock Images/Johnny Adolphson; p. 110 (BR): Alamy/©Juice Images; p. 111 (TR): Getty Images/Silvia Otte/Taxi; p. 111 (TL): Alamy/©IS831/Image Source; p. 111 (BL): Alamy/©pumkinpie; p. 111 (BR): Alamy/©Anatolii Babii; p. 112 (TL): Shutterstock Images/Jag_cz; p. 112 (TR): Shutterstock Images/Matteo photos; p. 112 (BL): Shutterstock Images/Lisa F. Young; p. 112 (BR): Alamy/©Sigrid Olsson/PhotoAlto; p. 113 (TL): Alamy/©David L. Moore - Lifestyle; p. 113 (BL): Shutterstock Images/OLJ Studio; p. 113 (TR): Corbis/David Lefranc; p. 113 (BR): Shutterstock Images/BKMCphotography; p. 114 (TR): Alamy/©John Elk III; p. 114 (TL): Shutterstock Images/Dja65; p. 115 (T): Getty Images/peplow/iStock/360; p. 117 (TR): Bridgeman Art Library / Musee Marmottan, Paris, France / Giraudon; p. 117(BL): Alamy/©Painting; p. 119 (TL): Alamy/©emanja Radovanovic; p. 120 (L1): Getty Images/Songquan Deng/iStock/360; p. 120 (L2): Getty Images/Matthew Dixon/iStock/360; p. 120 (R1): Alamy/©Geoff Marshall; p. 120 (R2): Shutterstock Images/Art Konovalov; p. 121 (TR): Getty Images/Christopher Futcher/iStock/360; p. 121 (CR): Shutterstock Images/febri ardi Antonius; p. 122 (C):Alamy/©Paul Lindsay; p. 122 (TC): Shutterstock Images/jaroslava V; p. 123 (TL): actionplus sports images; p. 123 (CL): Alamy/©Stephen Barnes/Sport; p. 124 (C): Getty Images/Matthew Stockman/Getty Images Sport; p. 125 (TL): Corbis/Lea Suzuki/San Francisco Chronicle; p. 125 (TR): Superstock/Science and Society/Science and Society; p. 125 (BR): Shutterstock Images/Serdiukov; p. 125 (CR): Shutterstock Images/Matusciac Alexandru; p. 125 (CL): Shutterstock Images/Viktor Prymachenko; p. 125 (BL): Shutterstock Images/Africa Studio.

The publishers are grateful to the following illustrators:
David Belmonte (Beehive Illustration): p. 116; Anni Betts p. 4, 38; Nigel Dobbyn (Beehive Illustration): p. 78; Mark Duffin p. 12, 116; Guy Pearce p. 35; Sean Tiffany p. 5; Q2A Media Services, Inc. p. 5, 14, 15, 24, 36, 37, 46, 47, 58, 68, 80, 90, 91, 118; Tony Wilkins p. 115, 118.

All video stills by kind permission of:
Discovery Communications, LLC 2015: p. 8(1, 2, 4), 11, 14, 18 (1, 2, 4), 21, 24, 30 (1, 2, 4), 33, 36, 40 (1, 2, 4), 43, 46, 52 (1, 2, 4), 55, 58, 62 (1, 2, 4), 65, 68, 74 (1, 2, 4), 77, 80, 84 (1, 2, 4), 87, 90, 115, 116, 117, 118, 119, 120, 121, 122.

Cambridge University Press: 7, 8 (3), 16, 18 (3), 26, 30 (3), 38, 40 (3), 48, 52 (3), 60, 62 (3), 70, 74 (3), 84 (3), 92.

Corpus
Development of this publication has made use of the Cambridge English Corpus (CEC). The CEC is a computer database of contemporary spoken and written English, which currently stands at over one billion words. It includes British English, American English and other varieties of English. It also includes the Cambridge Learner Corpus, developed in collaboration with the University of Cambridge ESOL Examinations. Cambridge University Press has built up the CEC to provide evidence about language use that helps to produce better language teaching materials.

The publishers are grateful to the following contributors:
Blooberry: concept design
emc design limited: text design and layouts
QBS Learning: cover design and photo selection
Ian Harker and Dave Morritt at DSound: audio recordings
Integra: video production
Nick Bruckman and People's TV: voxpop video production
Hart McCleod: video voiceovers
Anna Whitcher: video management
BraveArts, S.L: additional audio recordings
Getty Images: music
Vicki Anderson: Speaking and Writing pages
Debbie Owen and Alice Martin: Starter Unit
Jose Luis Jiménez Maroto, José María Ruiz Vaca, Ani Quiñones and Alice Martin: CLIL pages
Mick Green: Grammar Reference pages
Emma Szlachta: Editor & Vocabulary Bank
Debbie Owen and Alice Martin: Project pages
Diane Nicholls: Corpus research & Get it Right features